ACE THE JOB INTERVIEW

The Fundamental Skills Needed To Ace Any Job Interview!

By Robert Ritua, MBA, Job Coach

Library of Congress Control Number 2020907576

ISBN 978-1-7349841-1-8

<u>DEDICATION</u>

To my family, friends, and to those who have been asking me, "What are you doing with your time?"

CONTENTS

INTRODUCTION

"Give a man a fish and you feed him for a day. Teach a man to fish and you feed him for a lifetime." -Proverb

The hiring process most businesses use is designed to eliminate as many job applicants as possible to narrow their search for the most qualified candidate for the position. The objective for you as a job seeker is to make it through the selection and screening process.

Some of the topics covered in this book are communication and interpersonal skills, selling, emotional and ethical intelligence, critical thinking and problem-solving skills, impromptu speaking, and even business etiquette and honing your personality. These skills and professional values are the fundamentals to ace any job interview. Most other job interview books that I have read or have come across just briefly mention these professional values and soft skills, if they mention them at all. Use this book as a supplement to your library of materials to guide you throughout the job-seeking and screening process.

Although this book gives examples of answers to some common interview questions as well, the answers are not meant for you to memorize and use. The intent is to get you to tap into and apply some of your own professional values and skills to come up with your own unique and genuine answers so that you stand out from other potential candidates. This book will help you even more effectively utilize some of the professional values and skills you already possess to strategically and competitively interview with confidence and poise. Tapping into these skills and professional values will not only help in a job interview, but will also help you keep your job, as these are key traits that employers require an employee to have.

"Studies by Stanford Research Institute and the Carnegie Mellon Foundation among Fortune 500 CEOs have discovered that 75% of long-term job success resulted from soft skills and only 25% from technical skills." (1)

However, it is worth mentioning here that this does not mean that hard skills are not important. Hard skills are still necessary, Just because I am meticulous, pay attention to detail, can stay calm and cool headed in stressful situations, am coachable, and am able to have a steady hand when I use a scalpel doesn't necessarily makes me well qualified to perform the duties of a surgeon. You still need the knowledge and the know-how to be successful.

This book cannot teach you the specific knowledge and the technical skills needed for a job. If you are an auto mechanic or a registered nurse or even a lawyer, this book does not have the capacity to cover the education, training, and the technical skills for your profession. Besides, I am most likely not the subject-matter expert in your profession. You must assess yourself, your qualifications, and acknowledge your strengths and work on your weaknesses.
Most of you take the time to master your profession but you rarely take the time to master job interviews. You use your skills at home and at work. You should use your skills in a job interview, as well. Although this book may be considered an introductory course to the skills needed to ace any job interview, at the end of each

chapter, I also offer exercises or more suggested reading to help further enhance those skills. Everyone is great at something but there is always room for improvement; so personal growth is very important. Make it a habit to apply these skills on a consistent basis to continuously improve and be even more prepared for interviews.

The methods taught in this book are not 100% guaranteed to get you a job. Results vary according to the individual and circumstances. There are many different reasons -the methods you are using may not be working for you. It may be the amount of time and effort you spend preparing for the job interview, or your level of job interviewing skills such as your emotional intelligence, or your interpersonal and communication skills. It may be the way you conducted yourself in the job interview, the way you dressed or even how you were referred for the job. You may have even interviewed well but the employer elected to hire another candidate instead of you.

Because I cannot guarantee that you will dedicate your time and effort in continuously becoming even better in your professional values and soft skills, this book does not guarantee you will get a job. Only you can guarantee your success.

Throughout this book, I share with you some of my knowledge and expertise from my experience in workforce services, career and life coaching, serving in the military, and as a member of the Society for Human Resource Management (SHRM), a Graduate in Master

Business Administration (MBA), a Business Owner, and a previous Jobseeker.

If you need further job coaching or even resume development, please contact me for a special price discount offer for those of you who purchased this book.

I encourage you to visit my website and follow me in social media to share your experiences as well as to connect with and learn from other business professionals in the global community.

Wish you the best.
Robert Ritua, MBA, Job Coach

PART 1.

YOUR SKILLS IN COMMUNICATION

"The quality of your life is in direct proportion to how you effectively communicate." -Anthony Robbins

Communication is paramount to your success, including acing any job interview. After all, you will be communicating with a person or a group of people in a job interview. However, just having a conversation with an interviewer will not get you hired; you must communicate effectively to get hired.

There are many kinds of communication. Storytelling, selling, negotiating, and even dressing to impress, are all forms of communication. Although these skills in communication are intertwined with the professional values and other soft skills discussed in this book, the bulk of the fundamental skills to ace any job interview is covered in Part 1.

CHAPTER 1.

ATTITUDE & INTRAPERSONAL COMMUNICATION SKILLS

"Attitude is a little thing that makes a big difference." - *Winston Churchill*

Positive Attitude, Positive Environment

Your attitude can affect someone else's attitude and even change the energy of the room. Ever felt the room go dim when someone is being negative? That negative energy can be contagious. Soon, everyone else in the room will start being negative, as well.

Employers look for someone who has a positive outlook on things and can bring positive energy into the workplace. Some effects of positivity in the workplace include:
- Increase in high performance and productivity;
- Enhancement of or increase in collaboration, teamwork, and morale;
- Optimistic outlook when faced with challenges;
- Willingness to change, learn, try new things, and strive for excellence; and
- Trust and rapport between people in the workplace.

Here are some things you can do at a job interview to exude and cultivate positivity:
- Dress for success.

- Greet everyone you meet with a professional handshake and a pleasant smile.
- Sit up erect and exude confidence and enthusiasm.
- Be respectful and build rapport.
- Welcome and give constructive feedback.
- Provide an optimistic view of things.
- Avoid making negative comments or negative connotations.
- Give or share credit where credit is due in your stories of experience.
- Promote rewarding someone in public and reprimanding someone in private.
- Express appreciation and gratitude before leaving the interview.

Positive Mind Set, Positive Talk

Do you talk to yourself? Listen to how you communicate with yourself. Is it negative? Is it positive?

In a job interview, questions may be asked to see if you have a positive or optimistic outlook on things.
- How do you handle disappointment and setbacks?
- What is your greatest weakness?

Many of you may have read the book The Little Engine That Could by Watty Piper in elementary school. But some of you may have forgotten to apply the lessons from that story. The lessons are not just for children; they teach determination, perseverance, and persistence, all of which are vital to job seekers. The book also teaches life skills. In the story, the little engine was hauling heavy cargo through some of the toughest terrains and some of the people he passed by, including people he knew and his friends, were having doubts about his being able to reach his destination with such a heavy load. This may mirror life. Sometimes the people around you, including your friends and family, have doubts about you. You may have doubts yourself, and then the negative self-talk kicks in: "I can't do this. Who am I kidding? There's no way I can do this." But in the story The Little Engine That Could, even through the most challenging times, the Little Engine would say to himself, "I think I can," and he ended up reaching his destination. (1) You will need to bring that positive mindset to the job interview.

That positive mindset manifests by answering questions in a positive tone. You may be asked, "Tell me about a time when you had a disagreement with your supervisor or coworker?" The general rule to answering this type of question is to avoid giving a negative response. An example of a negative response would be, "I never could get along with my coworkers because we always ended up yelling at each other and criticizing each other's ideas." Having a positive outlook will help you respond to such questions in a more positive tone: "Although my coworkers and I sometimes disagreed, we always had an open line of open communication that allowed constructive criticism so that we could collaborate and brainstorm to come to an agreed upon method in solving a problem."

Confidence

In a job interview, you may also have concerns about what the interviewer will think of you, especially if you've been fired from a job, have a criminal record, gaps of employment, or only short-term job experience. With these concerns, you may start questioning yourself, creating self-doubt and, thus, losing confidence in yourself and your abilities.

According to most recruiters and Human Resources (HR) professionals I spoke to, one notable trait is a candidate's confidence level. A candidate's credibility can be backed up by their confidence and conviction. Some candidates may walk into the interview with confidence and then lose it during the interview. Some candidates may be confident in answering certain questions and not so confident in answering others. Interviewers are more likely to select those candidates who can maintain their confidence level throughout the interview. Thus, displaying confidence is key, even if you make a mistake or believe you answered a question poorly.

Preparation

Speakers and entertainers still get stage freight before appearing even after numerous rehearsal hours. It is ok to be nervous, even on a job interview; it shows you care about the interview and its outcome. The key is to control your nervousness. You can minimize that nervousness and increase your confidence through preparation.

One of the things to prepare for an interview is having a value proposition. A value proposition is a sales pitch you deliver in an interview to mention what you bring and how valuable you will be to the organization. We will dive more into detail on value proposition in Chapter 4. Although you may prepare for an interview by rehearsing your value proposition and some interview questions, it is even more important to exercise and sharpen your professional skills. Remember that the intent of rehearsing is to get you to tap into and apply some of these skills to come up with your own unique and genuine answers to stand out from other potential candidate.

Psych Yourself Up
Another way to minimize nervousness, reinforce your positive mind set and increase your confidence is by doing something each day to "psych" yourself up. Sports coaches use positive affirmations when coaching a player to get them psyched up. "You can do it! You're the best!" Some people use positive affirmations to build up their self-esteem. Others use visualization; they vividly see themselves being offered the job. Every morning, I devote some time to personal development and, in that time, I look for an inspiring or motivational quote to reflect upon to get started for the day. You may be the type of person who gets up in the morning listening to music to get you going. Maybe going to the gym and working out gets you pumped up. You can use this concept to ace interviews or even to improve in your profession once you're hired. Figure out what works for you to help gain and maintain your confidence.

Positivity & Handling Employer Concerns

The hiring process is designed to select the best candidate for the job by winnowing out all of the others. Job applicants often get interviewed by various levels of the company during the hiring process and, at each level, the company narrows the candidate pool.

What you say during an interview may cause the interviewer to harbor some suspicion, uneasiness, worry, or even fear and, when they have doubts about hiring you, they can exclude you from moving forward in the hiring process.

Having a positive mindset helps tremendously in what you say and how you say it in a job interview. By setting a positive mindset, you will soon realize that positive talk results and presenting a positive demeanor is the key to doing well in a job interview, especially when handling some of the interviewer's concerns.

However, you must also be consciously self-aware of what you are saying and how you are saying it.

TMI-Too Much Information

"Just be yourself" is one of the many pieces of advice people are given when they are preparing for a job interview. Yes, you should be genuine; however, there are some things about yourself that you should avoid mentioning in a job interview. Both good and bad things happen in your professional and personal lives. You tend to discuss your age, children, family, problems you are faced with, and even past "wild and crazy" experiences with friends and people you meet. Although you may think engaging in "small talk" and casual conversations with an interviewer can build rapport, which it can when done correctly, it can also work against you in a job interview.

A general rule of thumb is to keep every discussion at a job interview professional and relevant, even when you are building rapport.

So how much is too much information? It may be you are proud of raising your child or babysitting your niece or nephew, but unless you are applying for a childcare position or a job interacting with children, that discussion is likely to be irrelevant in a job interview. You will need to make a judgement call based on the "vibe" you are feeling at the interview. To play it safe, stick to the general rule of thumb of keeping every discussion at a job interview relevant and professional. You can still be genuine and human while conducting yourself in a professional manner. There are other ways to build rapport with an interviewer.

Be careful what information you voluntarily provide.
When asked: Do you have any events coming up in your life that will take time away from work? You may say: "I'm pregnant and in a couple of months, I will need some time off." Or you may say: "I need to pick up my kids from school in the afternoon." Or you may say: "I have a family vacation already scheduled in a couple of weeks that I would need to take time off from work for." Based on such answers, an employer will likely have concerns regarding your availability and scheduling flexibility.

Remember, their goal is to find the most qualified candidate for the position. It is not in the best interests of an employer to hire someone who will not be available to work when the position becomes available.

Where do you see yourself in five years? If you are applying for a job in office administration, you may answer, "I'm going to school to obtain my nursing degree and, in five years, I see myself as a registered nurse." This answer may make you appear to be someone who is not planning to stay with the company long-term since you are already planning to leave the company once you complete your education. The other not-so-obvious perception is that you may not have a flexible schedule since you mentioned you are currently going to school. An employer may be concerned about conflicts with the work schedule. Are you flexible to work any shift? Will attending school hinder you from going to work? Education is great but an employer's priority is to hire someone for a job position they need to fill. If that job position requires you to be available for any shift, an employer may not be flexible to work with you on scheduling.

The best way to address the concerns of the employer is to not disclose too much personal information, present yourself in a positive way, and discuss relevant content, emphasizing what makes you qualified and a great candidate for the job.

Play Devil's Advocate and Think Like the Employer
I previously discussed having a positive mindset; however, negative thoughts sometimes arise. Take the opportunity to look at such negative thoughts from a different perspective. Expose and examine your doubts so that you can strategize on how best to address such concerns at the job interview. If you have concerns about what the interviewer may think about you, play devil's advocate and look at these concerns from their perspective. Perhaps you were fired from a job, have a criminal record or have gaps of employment? Now, imagine you are the interviewer and addressing these concerns. What answer would allow you to continue considering the person being interviewed? What answer would relieve your concerns about such situations? Flip the perspective back to you and imagine how your previous employment issues could affect your job, the people in the workplace, or the company? Imagine how the conversation would play out. Play the "what if they ask me this" game and run through some scenarios. Think of a positive comeback to a negative concern.

Suggestions for Handling an Employer's Concerns

If You do not Have a High School Diploma

This is not a deal breaker. An employer may elect to hire someone with experience who does not have a high school diploma. I spoke with the general manager of an auto shop where the company normally prefers to hire experienced auto mechanics who possess a high school diploma and are certified by the National Institute for Automotive Service Excellence (ASE), the group that certifies professionals in the automotive repair and service industry. I had a client with more than twenty years of automotive repair experience gained from working on cars since he had been a teenager. However, he did not have a high school diploma, nor was he ASE certified. I referred my client to the general manager at the auto shop and, after an intensive interview focused mainly on auto repair questions, the general manager was very impressed with my client's experience and he hired him for the job.

Although some employers will hire candidates without high school diplomas, many employers want to know that the candidate can do some basic math calculations, read and write, and communicate with people, in addition to having the skills required by the position. Thus, having a high school diploma can create more job opportunities.

If you do not have a high school diploma, you will need to sell your experience and adaptability. Highlight some of your soft skills and professional values, including transferrable skills you gained from volunteering or from extra-curricular activities. There are jobs that may not require a high school diploma, but with fierce competition in the workforce, a diploma is an added benefit to an employer. If you are currently enrolled in a program to complete your high school education, mention that and provide a timeframe for when you expect to complete it.

If you Recently Completed High School or College
One of the concerns an employer may have when you are applying for a job right out of high school or college is work experience. To alleviate this concern, mention any jobs you held while receiving your education, including student-work programs, volunteering, active involvement with professional clubs and associations, or any internships you may have had. Mention the skills and experience you obtained from team projects and assignments you had while attending school and from participating in extracurricular activities. You must highlight your transferrable skills. Also, mention any relevant courses you have taken. For example, if you are applying for a paralegal position, mention that you have completed certain law courses and paralegal studies. Academic achievements such as graduating with a Summa Cum Laude or that you were on the Dean's list t are notable achievements worth mentioning, as well.

If an Employer Prefers a Candidate with a College Degree
If you do not have a college degree, an employer may be concerned about whether you have the knowledge,

skills, or experience necessary for the job. You will need to mention where did you gain those knowledge, skills, or experience. Perhaps you gained them from prior work experience, volunteering, self-study, or even your hobbies.

If you have completed some college courses but do not have a college degree, mention the relevant courses you've taken. For example, if you are applying for a human resource generalist position, mention that you completed a course in human resources. Also mention if you completed an internship or a work-related program.

If you are still attending college, mention that you are a current student and discuss your course of study and what you've learned so far. Mention if you are in an internship or work-related program. Remember to provide a timeframe of when you expect to complete your courses and obtain your degree.

If an Employer Prefers a Candidate Possess a Certain Certification

If you attended a trade school or have completed some type of vocational training, most employers may recognize those certifications, depending if the school's curriculum meets the federal, state, and industry standards. Employers may also offer training or educational assistance programs for certifications. For example, Walgreens offers their employees the opportunity to apply for the Pharmacy Educational Assistance Programs to become Pharmacists or Pharmacy Technicians (2). These certifications may also be transferrable with other employers in that industry. However, some employer's certification courses may be only recognized in-house and may not be transferrable. For example: When I served in the Navy, I was also trained as an armed sentry after completion of the armed sentry certification course. When I left the Navy and relocated to Las Vegas, NV, I was seeking employment during the recession in 2008. I was not aware that an armed and/or unarmed work card, also known as a guard card, was required to work as a security officer in the state of Nevada. My armed sentry certification was not transferrable. You will need to check with the state's licensing board as well as with the potential employer to see if the certification you have is acceptable. You may need additional certifications and/or professional licenses.

If you do not have the preferred certification, you will need to provide reassurance to the potential employer that you are either in the process of obtaining the certification with a timeframe when you expect to complete it or explain why you are worth the company's investment in providing you their certification course. You may incur the full cost of the certification or both you and the potential employer may share the cost.

If you do not have the funds to obtain the certifications, ask the potential employer if there are payment options for you. You may need to agree to an employment term contract with the company if the company incurs the cost for you to obtain certification or you may be able to setup a payment plan so that the cost can be deducted from your paycheck.

If the Job You are Applying for is not Your Ultimate Career Desire

If you are applying for a job that is not your ultimate career objective, you may want to keep your personal goal to yourself. Employers spend a lot of resources to get you hired and trained. Mentioning to an employer that you plan to be elsewhere in a couple of months or years may disqualify you from moving forward in the hiring process. Why would they spend their resources on you if you are already planning to leave? Always convey a positive message when you are asked why you are applying for the job.

You may have been told that you should do what you love or are passionate about. However, you may not able to do what you love at this moment. For example, if you want to become a doctor so that you can help and heal people, you may not be qualified to be a doctor right now and will need to go to medical school. You will need a job that you qualify for now in the interim.

An employer may be concerned about whether you have the enthusiasm for the job you are interviewing for. It may not be your dream job but if you can gain some satisfaction from what you are doing, employers may give you the opportunity. In the job interview, highlight what you would like about working there. Mention something about the job that would provide satisfaction and why you plan to do great work so an employer can appreciate having you on their team. You never know that job may later become a career for you or it can, at least, provide you with recommendations when you do leave the company.

If You Are Changing Careers

An employer may be concerned with whether you have the education and experience necessary for the new job. Ensure you do meet at least the minimum education requirements, including obtaining any certifications and licenses required for the job. Gain an understanding of the industry you are getting into. For example, if you are applying to work at a bank for the first time, research and be familiar with the general policies and procedures in banking. Highlight your transferrable skills and relevant work experience.

You Were Terminated from Your Previous Job

Employers may have some reservations from hiring you if you were terminated from your previous job. Employers may have doubts about your character or work performance, especially if you were terminated for not meeting a certain performance metrics such as sales quota or you did something serious that was against company policy. Always add a positive spin whenever you address why you were terminated to reassure to the potential employer that you have resolved and addressed any issues that caused your termination, such as habitual tardiness or absence, inability to resolve conflicts or disagreements with others, or inability to meet standards or follow instructions. Notice these reasons stem from the mismanagement of certain soft skills or professional values. You can build these skills up so that they are no longer an issue.

There could also be a situation in which you were wrongfully terminated. Regardless of the reason and nature of your termination, the interview is not the appropriate forum to play the blame game and vent your frustration. Always present yourself in a positive way, mention what lessons you learned, show enthusiasm for moving forward, and always emphasize why you are a great fit for the job.

If You Were Laid Off from Your Previous Job

Being laid off does not necessarily create a negative impression about you, especially if the company did a mass lay off. However, in the event it was only you who got laid off, an employer may question why you were chosen. It could be perceived that you were not an invaluable employee who was worth keeping. There are many factors that play into a company's decision to lay off employees. Some may have a seniority policy, which means they lay off junior personnel before they start laying off senior personnel. Regardless of the reason and nature of your lay off, an interview is not the appropriate time to start playing the blame game and venting your frustration. Always add a positive spin whenever you address why you were laid off such as the company needed to downsize or the company restructured and mention what lessons you gained or some of the achievements you accomplished during your tenure there.

If You Have Held Multiple Jobs, Each for a Short Period of Time

If you've mainly been a short-term employee, an employer may be concerned about your stability and maturity when considering you for the job. Were you let go prior to completing your probationary period? Did you work at several companies for only a short period of time? Having held multiple jobs, each for a short period of time, can be perceived as a pattern of instability. An employer may see a lack of focus, an uncertainty about your strengths, or a lack of understanding about what it is you enjoy doing. It can be perceived as though you are still in the process of finding yourself. Your commitment, work ethic, ability to work as a team member, and other professional values may all be called into question by an employer in such a situation. You will need to address these concerns head on. Display definite focus and commitment. Emphasize the strengths that are most relevant to the job and discuss your intention to stay and grow with the company.

Playing devil's advocate to think of a positive comeback to a negative concern was discussed earlier. In this instance, if you have held multiple jobs each for a short period of time, you could address the concern by saying something like: "Although I have held multiple jobs, I started working when I was in high school. I also worked while I was in college obtaining an Associate's Degree in accounting. Most of those jobs were seasonal. Having held various responsibilities has taught me different business-related skills, from customer service and sales to stocking and inventory to ecommerce order fulfillment. I am strong in math, well organized, and detail oriented, which is why I have decided to pursue a career in accounting and would be a great fit in your accounting department as an accounts receivable clerk."

If There are Gaps of Employment & You've Been out of the Workforce for a Time

Here are some reasons why someone may have gaps of employment and/or may have been out of the workforce for some time:

- Pregnancy/Maternity Leave (paid or unpaid),
- Stay-at-home parent/Homemaker, or
- Stay-at-home elderly care (taking care of your parents or grandparents).

In this situation, an employer may be concerned about your stability and work experience. You will need to convince employers that you have the skills and experience necessary to do the job by emphasizing how you gained those skills and experience. Refer to any of your previous jobs. Mention any activities you did while you were out of the workforce. Mention some of the transferable skills you applied during that time. It is best if you can back your statements up with proof. Mention if you went to school, completed some courses or obtained a degree, completed vocational training, attended seminars or workshops, or maybe even did some self-studying. Mention any volunteering and community service you contributed to or spent time doing. For example, fundraising is an example of applying your sales experience, as well as your money-handling and recordkeeping skills. Tell a story about a time when you applied what you learned or your skills. Display definite focus and commitment. Emphasize the strengths that are most relevant to the job and your intention to stay and grow with the company.

If You Are a Military Veteran

To show verification that you served in the military, you may be required to provide employers with a copy of your DD-214 or discharge papers. This document will mention things like the dates of your time in service, your rank and job title, and the character of discharge, which lets employers know whether you were discharged in good terms or not.

An employer may wonder how to apply what you did in the military to relevant work experience. When I served in the U.S. Navy, my job title was an Aviation Machinist Mate, also known as an Aircraft Engine Mechanic in the private sector. However, I also held other positions such as Shop Manager, Shift Supervisor, Quality Assurance Representative, and even Security Officer. If you are a military veteran, the challenge for you is to translate military jargon into a language an employer understands.

The military uses a lot of acronyms and as a veteran myself, I don't even know the meaning of most of them. Imagine how an employer feels when you start speaking military jargon; they will most likely be confused. Even if the interviewer is also a military veteran, they still may not necessarily understand the jargon you use since each branch of the armed forces has its own jargon. For example, a job title in the private sector, is called a MOS (Military Occupational Specialty Code) by the Army and called Rate by the Navy. So, when someone asks me what my MOS is, they are asking me, "What is your job title?"

Prior to the interview, research and learn about the company's industry, as well as any industry-specific language so that you can translate your military jargon into theirs.   Find a way to relate your military responsibilities and duties to the responsibilities and duties of the job you are applying for. More information about researching companies is provided in Chapter 4.

Mention any relevant courses and training you took while you served in the military. Some certifications and licenses from the military can also be used in the private sector but you may need additional certifications for civilian work.

Employers may offer you a job contingent upon obtaining the required certifications and licenses. As a veteran, you may be eligible for education benefits such as the GI Bill. For more information visit the Education and Training Page on the United States Department of Veterans Affairs (VA) Website:
https://www.benefits.va.gov/gibill/ (3)

Some veterans may have a health condition that is also considered a service-connected disability. However, an employer may not recognize the condition as a disability because the military rates service-connected disabilities to calculate compensation; similar to workers' compensation if you work in the private sector. Some health conditions are considered presumptive from service if criteria are met.

For example, if a veteran served in the Vietnam War, he or she may have been exposed to Agent Orange. The United States Department of Veterans Affairs (VA) presumes some health conditions and disabilities were caused by Agent Orange and other herbicide exposure, such as Chronic B-Cell Leukemia, Type 2 Diabetes, Hodgkin's Disease, Prostate Cancer, Respiratory Cancers, and Parkinson's Disease. (4)

Another such example includes Gulf War veterans who have served since August 2, 1990, who may develop health conditions due to possible environmental exposure. Gulf War veterans may contact the VA Environmental Health Coordinator about getting a Gulf War Registry Health Exam. (5)

For more information visit The Public Health page of The United States Department of Veterans Affairs (VA) Website: https://www.publichealth.va.gov/ (6)

When given the job offer, you may also provide them with a copy of your rating disability letter. This can provide the employer clarification to your disability.

If You Have a Disability
There are laws protecting those with disabilities. Employers are not to discriminate a job candidate based on their disability although, employers do need to know that you can perform the job duties. We will discuss handling discrimination later in this chapter. If you have a disability, know your capabilities and whether you can perform the job duties with or without reasonable accommodations. During the job interview, highlight your abilities and avoid discussing what you are unable to do. When you are given the job offer, you can provide a copy of medical documents to the employer so that the

employer knows the specific accommodations you may need. Despite providing this information, you may also be required to undergo a physical test and/or medical examination as part of an employer's hiring process. For example, some professions such as law enforcement officers and firefighters will need to pass a physical test and complete a medical examination, including a drug test as part of the hiring process.

If You Are 50+ Years of Age
In the 2015 movie <u>The Intern</u>, a seventy-year-old baby boomer was hired to work as a senior intern at an online fashion company founded and managed by a millennial. The movie is a great depiction of the contrast between the work environment of baby boomers and the modern workplace. (7).

Because of such major changes in the workplace, an employer may be concerned about an older candidate's adaptability and coachability. Such candidates may not take instructions well, especially if given by someone who is younger or with less work experience than they have. Having many years of experience does not necessarily translate to adaptability. For example, if you have been driving for many years, you may consider yourself an experienced driver. Do you remember when you first learned to drive, where you had to position your hands? Did you place your hands at the ten o' clock and 2 o' clock positions? Where are your hand positions when you drive now? Be honest. Do you continue to drive with your hands at the ten o' clock and 2 o' clock positions or do you drive with one hand? After years of driving, you tend to develop bad habits in your driving skills. The same concept holds true with work experience. You may be set in your own ways when it comes to doing certain things. To an employer, you may appear to be difficult to retrain.

Another challenge an older candidate may face is being up to date with the technology of today. Computers are used in all types of businesses to operate efficiently. Walk into a well-established auto-shop chain like PEP Boys, and you will notice even in the auto industry, computers are being used. Customer-service representatives answer phone calls in a call center utilizing computers to input data, as well as to navigate around the company's customer-management system. If you are 50+ years of age, you may have experience in bookkeeping, but you may not be familiar with modern bookkeeping programs. Employers tend to think that a stereotypical 50+ job candidate may not be as proficient in using computers, email, or may not utilize mobile phone apps like many millennials do.

Fortunately, there are laws protecting 50+ candidates from discrimination. Therefore, some employers may assess a job candidate's computer skills by requiring an online application and communication via email. So, if you are 50+, you will need to convince employers that you are adaptable and coachable in addition to keeping up with the hard skills required in the modern age. Being adaptable and coachable is also covered in Chapter 9.

Handling Discriminatory or Criminal Background Inquiries

I've had several job applicants tell me that in some of their interview experiences, they have been asked inappropriate and illegal questions. This topic is vast enough to require a book all on its own so I will do my best to provide some basic information to help you strategize how best to address such questions.

Although there are laws to protect applicants from discrimination, discriminatory acts may occur, unintentionally or intentionally. Some interviewers may not be trained or knowledgeable in the laws regarding what they can legally ask in a job interview.

Some questions that are discriminatory are:
- What is your age?
- Where were you born?
- Are you married?
- Are you pregnant?
- Do you have any children?
- Are you an ex-felon?

When asked a question that is discriminatory, you could:
- Be cooperative, answer the question, and hope the information you provide will not be used as part of the employer's decision to hire you.
- Point out that the question is discriminatory but be cooperative and answer the question anyway.
- Point out that the question is discriminatory and choose not to answer the question basing the refusal on the basis that it requests private/personal information that is irrelevant to the job.

- Point out that the question is discriminatory and proceed to file a formal complaint and pursue a discrimination lawsuit against the interviewer.

When asked a question that is discriminatory or inappropriate, you may want to reconsider whether you want to work for the company considering the type of work environment you may be getting yourself into. It may not be worth the aggravation and stress you could feasibly go through every day, not to mention the assumption of continued harassment and discrimination. Remember, when you are in the interview, you have the opportunity to assess the company culture and determine whether you can thrive in the company's work environment or not.

Ban the Box and The Fair Chance Act

Besides federal legislation, states in the U.S. also have their own legislation and criminal justice policies regarding discrimination.

In an article titled, "Ban the Box: U.S. Cities, Counties, and States Adopt Fair Hiring Policies", written by Beth Avery and the National Employment Law Project (NELP), updated on July 1, 2019, on the NELP's website, it stated that "Nationwide, 35 states and over 150 cities and counties have adopted what is widely known as 'ban the box' so that employers consider a job candidate's qualifications first, without the stigma of a conviction or arrest record. These initiatives provide applicants a fair chance at employment by removing the conviction history question from job applications and

delaying background checks until later in the hiring process." Here is the link to read the full article: https://www.nelp.org/publication/ban-the-box-fair-chance-hiring-state-and-local-guide/
(8)

Although an employer may not inquire about your criminal background, at least not until a job offer is made, the employer still may elect not to hire someone with a criminal record once the background check has been completed. It is legal for a company not to hire someone with a criminal record so long as the company is consistent in the application of their hiring procedures. Any inconsistencies in their procedures may be considered discriminatory.

When employers inquire about a job candidate's criminal background, the type and content of such questions depends on the job itself and the state where the business is located. For example, laws in some states do not allow an employer to ask questions about arrests. Contact your state equal employment agency for more information.

If you do have any convictions, including any traffic violations that resulted in a misdemeanor conviction, ensure you know the details of your charges. You should at least know:
- The classification and level of each of your convictions: Is it a misdemeanor, gross misdemeanor, or felony conviction? If so, what category or level is the conviction?
- The date of the arrest and the date of being charged with the conviction.

- Details of your sentencing: Were you required to pay a fine? Were you required to complete community service? If so, did you complete it? Did you undergo rehabilitation or treatment? Were you incarcerated? If so, what were the dates of your incarceration? What are/were the dates of your parole?
- Is your court case open or closed? Do you have an open warrant?

Note: Obtain the aforementioned information if you do not know or have forgotten. It's understandable that you may want to put your past to rest and revisiting the past can be traumatic and painful, but knowing the details is important when applying for jobs.

Offer an Explanation

If a potential employer offers you a job offer then inquire about your criminal history, provide with a letter of explanation with relevant documents.

Here are some guidelines to follow when explaining your convictions to a potential employer:

- Be honest. Do not lie about your criminal history. There have been numerous cases in which job applicants lied about their criminal background and were not hired because of their non-disclosure. In such cases, the employers didn't exclude applicants based on their criminal record, but rather, on the fact that the applicants lied, which made them seem untrustworthy. Remember, you are being considered to join an organization and trust plays a major role in the hiring decision.

- Be careful not to volunteer too much information. Provide only the facts, including the resolution of the case and if it has since been closed. Even if you are upset by the outcome of the charges, it is not the time or place to vent your frustrations to the potential employer. The employer was not the judge or jury on your case and cannot change the outcome of your case.
- Humble yourself, take responsibility, and own up to your mistakes. Display that you are not living in the past. Mention what you have learned from your mistakes and what changes have you made since then to move forward in your life.

*Companies may also have their own policies and guidelines for evaluating a potential candidate's credit history. You may have been laid off from your previous job, been a victim of mortgage fraud, or had to file for foreclosure, but it's not the time or place to bring up or argue about these issues either. Instead, try to influence the potential employer to re-evaluate their guidelines by making a compelling case regarding your circumstances. If a potential employer does inquire about your credit history, provide a letter of explanation and don't forget to include what you have done or what you are doing to correct the problem.

So, What Jobs Do You Qualify with Your Criminal Record?

You may have met your court-ordered requirements, accepted the consequences of your actions, and paid your debt to society; however, your convictions may still hinder you from holding certain positions in a workplace.

Your past criminal history plays a big factor in an employer's decision to hire you. If you have a consistent criminal history, employers may believe that you have not moved on from your criminal past, especially if you have an open case or a current warrant for your arrest. Alternately, employers may perceive a single, past criminal conviction as a life-changing event that you have learned and moved on from.

Until you can get your record sealed or expunged, you will need to take a realistic and honest look at yourself and be open to the jobs that are available to you. To change your life around, you will likely need to accept jobs you may not necessarily want to do but can qualify for. Be realistic with your job expectations.

One way to determine whether you will qualify for a position is to compare the details of your crime to the duties of a position. Employers will not hire someone with a criminal record if it opens them up to liability. Employers have the legal obligation to ensure safety within their organization and for their customers. If the criminal record is directly related to the responsibilities and duties of the job, you will most likely be disqualified for that specific position. For example, if your criminal record indicates that you were convicted of stealing money or check or credit fraud, you will most likely be disqualified from working as a bank teller or a cage cashier at a casino because the job duties entail being entrusted with handling large sums of money. Someone with a criminal record for criminal acts of violence, spousal or child abuse, or battery and assault will likely not be selected for a job that involves the public's safety. By asking questions about your criminal history, employers can prevent a lawsuit against their business for negligent hire.

Keep an open mind; you may be qualified for jobs not directly related to your criminal conviction that you never thought of. One of my clients had a great job as an IT tech prior to being convicted of a felony. His felony record disqualified him to return to work as an IT tech because he would have had access to company computers and confidential information. Thus, hiring an IT tech with a felony record would create liability. Because it takes time to get a record sealed or expunged, my client decided to focus on training for a different career. He sought my services and, after he completed vocational training in culinary arts, he obtained a job as a kitchen worker at one of the restaurants in Las Vegas.

Here are some resources for further information regarding background checks:

Article: "Background Checks, What Employers Need to Know." U.S. Equal Employment Opportunity Commission (EEOC).
www.eeoc.gov/eeoc/publications/background_checks_employers.cfm

- This is a joint publication by the EEOC and the Federal Trade Commission (FTC) that covers what employers need to know regarding background checks. (9)

Article: "Pre-Employment Inquiries and Arrest & Conviction." EEOC.
www.eeoc.gov/laws/practices/inquiries_arrest_conviction.cfm
It covers:

- Employment decisions that may violate Title VII of the Civil Rights Act of 1964, as amended (Title VII)
- The Difference Between Arrest Records and Conviction Records
- Consumer Protections and Criminal Background Checks (10)

Book: The New Scarlet Letter? Negotiating the U.S. Labor Market with a Criminal Record by Steven Raphael.

Website: "BanTheBoxCampaign.org"
http://bantheboxcampaign.org/
This website contains more information about the Ban the Box Campaign.

Here are some suggested books for further information in the area of personal development:

Awaken the Giant Within: How to Take Immediate Control of Your Mental, Emotional, Physical and Financial Destiny! by Anthony Robbins

Mindset by Carol Dweck

Positions of Power: Using the Body to Harness the Power of the Mind by Amy Cuddy

The Keys to Success by Jim Rohn

The Power of Positive Thinking by Dr. Norman Vincent Peale

The Success Principles by Jack Canfield

Unlimited Power by Anthony Robbins

177 Mental Toughness Secrets of the World Class by Steve Siebold

CHAPTER 2.

YOUR COMMUNICATION SKILLS

"To effectively communicate, you must realize that you are all different in the way you perceive the world and use this understanding as a guide to our communication with others." -Tony Robbins

When communicating with someone, you use one or a combination of these three modes of communication:
- Visually (body language, gestures, postures, and facial expressions),
- Vocally (tone of voice) and/or
- Verbally (words).

Visual Mode of Communication

Ever played charades? Your movements and facial expressions give clues to the other players so they can determine what you are trying to convey without verbally saying it. Actions speak louder than words. Knowing how to say something and what to say in a job interview are just as important as the way you deliver the message. You must also use these skills to interpret the messages the interviewer is communicating to you.

You use words, punctuation, and even emojis to create meaning in your texts, messages, emails or posts on social media. A painting without the words can also convey a message, hence the saying, "A picture is worth a thousand words." Similarly, you can also convey messages via body language and/or facial expressions when conversing.

You all understand body language to some extent. You can identify if a person is happy, sad, or angry by observing their facial expressions and body language. For example, non-verbal clues such as pounding your fist on a table demonstrate that you are angry.

Society and culture can also create standards of communication using body language, such as American Sign Language, a wave or other widely recognized languages and gestures. For example, when I was in the Navy as an Aircraft Engine Mechanic, I also was a qualified Plane Captain, the person who would direct the pilot when parking the aircraft just after landing. The pilot would be in the cockpit and I would be outside the aircraft where there would also be a lot of other noise, making verbal communication ineffective. Instead, we used certain designated hand signals or used lighted wands at night to communicate with each other.

Paying attention to the interviewer's verbal and non-verbal cues will help you:
- Understand the message the interviewer is conveying.
- Get a feel for how the interviewer thinks you handled the interview questions. Were you able to persuade the interviewer to seriously consider you for the position?
- Get a feel for whether you and the interviewer have created some type of rapport. Having built good rapport can make the conversations in the

interview a lot more comfortable, if not easier, for the both of you.

Note: Remember that the interviewer is likely reading you, as well. Be mindful of your body language and how the two of you are communicating non-verbally.

The Handshake
In general, physical contact can enhance communication. How much and what kind of contact is acceptable depends on the situation, culture, and relationship of the parties. When appropriate, making physical contact with others can help them feel more comfortable and receptive to you.

In a job interview, however, a handshake is just about the only light physical contact that is culturally acceptable. Traditionally, a handshake in America is a welcoming gesture and, in a business environment, it is a form of business etiquette and professionalism. Other forms of physical contact during an interview can be inappropriate and may be perceived as offensive or harassment.

A firm handshake with direct personal eye contact conveys a message of confidence and respect. A handshake is one of those little things that make a big difference. Try this exercise whenever you are networking with other people: shake the hand of each person that you meet with a different style. You could deliver a soft handshake with one person and a firm handshake with another. Notice how they react and interact with you afterwards. Make note of those styles that garner positive attention and avoid the others when interviewing.

Social   Norm   Update: Covid-19/Coronavirus Pandemic Social Distancing
As of this writing, the global economy is experiencing the Covid-19/Coronavirus Pandemic and social distancing is one of the precautionary measures people are taking to mitigate the spread of the virus. If social distancing continues, the rules for handshakes may change. Handshakes will no longer be required, and in fact, may be unacceptable.   In addition, interviewers and interviewees may choose to use some type of facemask for further protection.   We may see employers conducting video-conferencing interviews rather than in-person.

Rest assured, whether the interview is through video-conferencing or in-person, you can still deliver a pleasant greeting and introduction without a handshake just by maintaining eye contact and having a pleasant smile. Your tone of voice changes with a smile. If you meet in person, but are both wearing facemasks, you can still feel the positive and pleasant energy. Plus, when you have a genuine smile on your face, it reaches your eyes.

Eye Contact
In a job interview, maintaining eye contact conveys the message that you respect the other person, are interested and focused on the conversation, and are confident in yourself. So, give eye contact but avoid the

serial-killer stare. If you feel awkward with direct eye contact, a strategy that may help is to imagine a triangle with one point of the triangle at the top of the person's head and the other two points located at either end of the person's eyes. Look into the middle of the triangle, which is the person's forehead or the top of the nose. From a distance of approximately 3 feet away or more, it will appear that you are maintaining eye contact with the person you are having a conversation with while alleviating your discomfort.

Facial Expressions
In a job interview, watch the interviewers' facial expressions as you answer questions. If he or she appears confused, you need to adjust and modify your answers, perhaps clarifying what you just said. You could also ask the interviewer to restate the question; perhaps you misunderstood what he or she was asking you. However, some interviewers may give you a blank look, like a professional poker player not giving away any emotion. You may be unable to read his or her emotions easily. In such situations, pay attention to body language and tone of voice to make an overall assessment of what the interviewer is conveying to you. Just a reminder, the interviewer will simultaneously be watching your facial expressions and body language to read you.

Remember, you express your feelings through facial expression. You want to express openness, confidence, and enthusiasm in an interview. There may be times, however, when a poker face is more beneficial, such as when you are negotiating your salary and other benefits packages.

Have a Pleasant Smile

In an article entitled "You Can't Train a Smile", written by the founder of the Virgin Group Richard Branson, which was posted on the company's website on April 03, 2015, Richard talked about hiring people who like to smile. He had a discussion with Nicholas Peluffo and Nicholas's father, Daniel, both of whom built a hotel company. Daniel pointed out that the smiles of their employees make a key difference. Daniel said, "As an employer, you can train your staff in every single other skill you need. You can train them to learn new techniques or do different jobs. You can train them on what to do and what to say. But you can't train a smile." Richard agreed and said, "A smile can prompt a smile, extend into a laugh, and bring happiness to an entire room. When somebody smiles at you, it is immediately clear whether the smile is genuine or forced. You can tell if the person's eyes shine and their whole face lights up, or if their lips simply upturn a little. You can tell if the person is happy and sharing their happiness with you. This is untrainable." (1)

Postures and Gestures

In a job interview, be mindful of gestures that may create barriers, such as crossing your arms, turning your body at an oblique angle or even placing your briefcase on your lap in front of you when having a discussion with the interviewer. Gestures that create barriers can convey a feeling of insecurity, shyness, or even make you appear closed off or untrustworthy, as if you have something to hide. Further, depending on how big the barrier is, it could hinder eye contact, which is crucial in building rapport and communicating effectively.

You can communicate using hand gestures without actually using sign language. Use hand gestures to enhance the meaning of a message. For example, you could hold up three fingers on one hand while counting each finger with the other to highlight three points you are discussing in a job interview. If you know the employer prefers to hire a candidate who has more than 4 years of experience, you could hold up five fingers to give a visual image of your years in the business to emphasize that you meet the requirement. However, avoid overusing hand movements. Some people speak with their hands so excessively that it becomes a distraction. Further, hand movements at eye level create a barrier, breaking eye contact with the interviewer.

Confidence

Since you do not sit through job interviews daily, the experience can be intimidating and even stressful. Nervousness can set in. Some signs of nervousness are:

- Shaking your legs.
- Tapping your feet or even tapping something you are holding, such as a pen.
- Swinging your body from left to right when seated in a chair that swivels.

- Grooming or playing with your hair, or your clothes and accessories, such as a tie or a piece of jewelry.
- Scratching or rubbing a body part such as your chin, nose, or fingertips.
- Shaky voice.

You can change from feeling powerless to feeling powerful and confident just by making some adjustments to your posture. You can even use power poses as non-verbal communication with yourself to trigger chemicals in your brain to boost confidence. For example, you can make a powerful statement and increase your level of confidence just by standing and putting your hands on your hips, posing like Superman or Wonder Woman.

Energy and Enthusiasm
Body language tells more about your state of mind than facial expressions do. You come across as depressed when there is a lack of energy in your movement or when your posture droops. You demonstrate enthusiasm when you are full of energy, have an erect posture or movements that are more upbeat, maybe even hyperactive. You can sense a person's emotions and state of mind just by observing the changes in their energy levels.

In a job interview, maintain your professional demeanor but supplement it with your excitement and enthusiasm. Avoid slouching or even displaying a look of boredom. You do not want to come across as being uninterested in the job or uninterested in joining the team and the organization. Alternately, you should not act overly excited, which could translate into being desperate for a job. Such behavior may hinder you from strategizing effectively when negotiating your salary and other incentives.

Using "Props" to Enhance Your Communication
On a day-to-day basis, you may use your tattoos, hair style, clothing, and other accessories, to communicate your personality the way actors use props to enhance their message.

In a job interview, however, displaying your tattoos or your faddish green hair may not be an appropriate message to convey. You must research the company and its culture. Some companies may support expressing yourself in such a way, while others may not. Realize that in a job, you may have to conform to meet company expectations. Being yourself at home and at work are two different things. At work, you must be your professional self. Putting your feet up having a laptop on your lap while watching T.V. at home may be comfortable, but you probably shouldn't behave that way when you are at work.

The clothes you wear in a job interview can also convey a message about your character. Appropriate attire for a job interview conveys the message that you are prepared, serious about the job, and can present yourself in a professional manner. Refer to "First Impressions Through Your Wardrobe" in Chapter 6 for more information about wardrobe choices.

You can also use props, such as a pointer, when delivering a presentation to your interviewers to enhance your communication. By doing so, you convey the message that you are well organized and proud of your achievements. Make sure to display some of your more notable accomplishments if you do decide to compile a professional portfolio or PowerPoint presentation. Refer to "Using Visual Aids in Your Interview Sales Presentation" in Chapter 4 for more information.

If you do have things to share from your portfolio, such as your resume or letters of recommendation, have extra copies to hand out. You may be in a panel interview with two or more interviewers and you want to be sure to have a copy for each. Also have hard copies of your PowerPoint presentation in case there are technical or computer problems or are in a place where PowerPoint is not available.

Be ready to discuss the details in your professional portfolio, PowerPoint presentation, or on your resume. If you have a copy of an achievement award to show and tell, be ready to tell the story of how you obtained that achievement award. Also, be ready for any follow-up questions that may arise. Refer to "Using Visual Aids in Your Interview Sales Presentation", "Selling and Storytelling", "Topics You Should Discuss", and "Questions You Should Ask" in Chapter 4 for more information.

Vocal and Verbal Mode of Communication

Your Phraseology

How you phrase things in a job interview matters. For the interviewer, it is inappropriate and illegal to ask a job candidate, "Are you pregnant?" Using appropriate phraseology can make all the difference: "Do you have any events coming up in your life that will take time away from work?" Similarly, you can portray a more positive image of yourself just by using certain words. You may seem unstable if you say that you worked a few months here and a few months there for several fast food restaurants. You can leave a more positive impression by saying that you have been in the fast-food service industry for over 5 years.

Avoid rambling on and on just to avoid awkward silences if the interviewer takes notes during the interview. You may talk your way out of getting hired if you divulge too much unnecessary information. The quality of what you say is more important than the quantity of what you say, so make the words you do say count.

Some people try to use new words that don't suit their personality or that are misused in the context of a sentence. You should not use words that are not in your everyday vocabulary during a job interview. Prior to a job interview, you can work on improving your vocabulary by familiarizing yourself with terminology for the job. For example, some companies use different job titles for the same thing. In hospitality, some hotels use the job title Housekeeper, while others use the term Guest Room Attendant. Hotels use the job title Porter, while schools use the job title Custodian. As you improve your vocabulary, you will notice the new words you learn will be easier to incorporate into your everyday language, making you sound more authentic when using them.

Speak with Clarity: Pronunciation and Enunciation

Speaking with clarity involves both pronouncing words correctly and enunciating words clearly and concisely, instead of mumbling or slurring the words. Here are some commonly mispronounced words:

Word	Mispronunciation	Enunciation
Especially	Ex-specially	Es-pecially
Espresso	Ex-presso	Es-presso
February	Feb-uary	Feb-ru-ary
Library	Lib-ary	Lib-rary
Often	Off-ten	Off-en (silent "t")

Speaking a Different Language

Employers may be looking for a candidate who can speak a foreign language, such as Spanish, Japanese, or Chinese. In a job interview for such a position, you may be asked to speak the foreign language as a test. Be sure to mention your level of fluency in the language, i.e. whether you can only speak and understand it but not write it.

What about Profanity?

Some people may have the habit of using profanity in their everyday language, "F*** this and F*** that." However, it is unprofessional to use profanity, especially in a job interview, a business communication or when marketing yourself on social media. Refer to the topic about branding in Chapter 6 and "What About Using Profanity" in Chapter 8.

Vocal Variety

Depending on how you convey your story—pitch, pauses, pace, volume, and tone— you can demonstrate different emotions and pique interest. In a job interview, you should add some vocal variety when you are telling a story, especially if you want the interviewer to stay interested. Yes, storytelling. You should tell a story every time you are asked a question about a time in your past, such as, "Tell me a time when you had to deal with a difficult problem." Storytelling is discussed further in Chapter 4.

Pauses

You can use pace and pauses to enhance your communication, as well. How quickly or slowly you respond can send a message. A rushed answer can indicate urgency or maybe even desperation, such as quickly saying yes to a certain salary when given a job offer. When you are slow to respond, you may be conveying a message of hesitation or uncertainty. However, adding a pause to your conversation can have a dramatic effect.

It's also ok to pause and have a moment of silence to gather your thoughts before you speak. It can show that you stay calm in stressful situations and can even show your level of intelligence, by demonstrating that you gather your thoughts before explaining them. Using pauses in the proper place in your speech can make an impact in your message. However, pausing for too long after a question is asked implies that you have difficulty answering that particular question, which can cause concern on the part of the interviewer.

Utterances
Some of us tend to say "ah," "uh" and "um," as fillers for what would otherwise be a moment of silence; often they are used when you get nervous and are thinking of what to say next. Avoid consistent use of these filler words in a job interview. Overuse of fillers shows your nervousness, uncertainty, and unpreparedness.

Tone of Voice brings meaning, even to utterances
Tone does not just affect your words; it can also bring meaning to your utterances. For example, "Oh" takes on different meanings depend on how you say it. You can say "Oh" with a vocal tone, facial expression, and body gesture to convey surprise, fright, or even joy. Learn to pick up on utterances that relate to tone or pronunciations that seem unusual to you. Perhaps the person you are interviewing with has an accent. Utterances are subtle aspects of speech that help you understand what the interviewer is saying, especially when they speak with an accent or speak little to no English.

Customs and Cultures

Not only does language differ between countries, but there are also unique customs and cultural differences to take into consideration when you communicate with others. In Asia for example, people customarily greet each other with a bow, whereas in the United States people greet each other with a handshake. In the state of Hawaii, a Hawaiian or "Aloha" shirt can be considered business casual and culturally acceptable in the workplace, though it is usually deemed too casual on the mainland. This does not only apply to companies outside of your region, as a Japanese company in the U.S. may incorporate Japanese norms into their corporate culture, so be sure to do your research before going to the job interview. You may need to bow as they do in Japan to show respect as well as to show that you can assimilate with the people in the company.

In the 2013 comedy movie, The Internship, two middle-aged salesmen find themselves in the midst of a forced career change when technology makes their prior positions redundant. They applied to and were accepted into the internship program at Google. The movie offers a glimpse of the workplace environment at Google and how these two older interns need to update their skills to compete.(2) The movie is a great example of the need to be adaptable and to being open to working in a different work environment with a unique culture.

Company culture should play a major role in your decision to work for an organization. It determines not only whether you can perform your job well, but also, whether you can advance and thrive in the company's work environment. When preparing for a job interview, research everything about the position as well as about the company, including any information you can get about the company culture, the workplace environment, the people who work there, and the company's policies and procedures. As part of your research, visit the company if you can, to get a glimpse and a feel of the work environment. You can also interview some of the staff in the company to gauge how they feel about working there. Refer to "Needs Analysis" in Chapter 4 for more information.

Just as you research a company, an employer may do a background check on you. They can then make some assumptions based on those results along with the information provided on your application, resume, your social media profile, or from what they were told in recommendations and referrals. An employer uses a job interview to get a feel for whether you can fit in and thrive within their company culture. Part of their decision-making process is using their emotions and even their intuition or gut instinct to determine how they think and feel about you. Pay attention to how you brand and sell yourself.   Be sure to work to build rapport in the interview.   Show that you can adapt and assimilate. Refer to "Interpersonal Communication Skills" in Chapter 3, "Adaptable" in Chapter 9, and "Marketing Skills" in Chapter 6.

Methods of Communication
and Types of Job Interviews

There are a lot of methods you use to communicate: phone, email, video-conferencing, audio or video recording, social media, blogging, "snail" mail, presenting and delivering a speech or sales presentation on a stage, or even direct personal contact.

There are also various methods of interviewing that employers may use to conduct their screening and selection process. When you are contacted for an interview, ensure it is scheduled for an appropriate and mutually arranged time. You may not be as prepared as you want to be if you get an unexpected call to conduct a same-day or on-the-spot interview.

When scheduling an interview, ask:
- What date, time, and location will the interview be?
- Who will you be meeting with? (Get their names and positions, including the person you talked to on the phone.)
- How long will the meeting take and is there anything in the agenda you need to know about in advance? (Such information will help you prepare for what to discuss in the interview.)
- What was on your application or resume that caught their interest? (This information will help you know what to highlight in the interview.)
- What else do you need to bring, such as list of references, Letters of Recommendation, etc.

Phone/Video-Conferencing Interviews

You may be asked to start with a phone or video-conferencing interview before moving on to an in-person interview. You should treat a phone or video-conferencing interview the same as any other type of interview: with preparation.

Here are some pointers for when your interview is a phone or video-conferencing interview:

- Ensure you have the appropriate equipment. You will need, at minimum, a video camera, speakers, microphone, access to the internet, and access to a video-conferencing platform such as Skype or Zoom. It can be difficult to communicate effectively when there is intermittent transmission.

- If you plan on using your phone, ensure you use a phone stand to keep the visual display steady and to give yourself the ability to communicate with hand gestures.

- Consider where you will want to conduct the interview. If the room is too empty, there may be an echo that can be difficult to hear over from the other end.

- Consider what can be seen and heard on video. Dress for success. Use appropriate lighting and background. Avoid having pictures of your children displayed in the background. Ensure you deliver a good first impression.

- Avoid distractions. Turn off radios, televisions, and other noise-making distractions. Also avoid having other people around during your interview. They may be a distraction, especially if you have children or noisy pets.

Group Interviews

You may be pitted against other candidates during the job interview; you may even have to compete with them in front of the interviewers. Alternately, there could be a task that you need to complete with the other candidates, demonstrating your teamwork skills.

Here are some pointers for group interviews:

- Stay focused. Other candidates may cause distractions. Maintain your focus.
- Listen to the questions carefully and avoid self-doubt. You may listen to other candidates answer and it can be tempting to use similar responses, especially if you think their answers were well received. But you may have a better answer. Go with your gut. Never doubt yourself. Be confident in yourself and show conviction in your answers. Show that you can look at things from a different perspective.
- If you are in teams, and each team is to complete a certain task, show your team spirit. Be a team player, even though you may have assumed or were given a leadership role. Show off your communication skills and how well you work with others.

Panel Interviews & One-on-One Interviews

You may be interviewed by just one individual or by a panel of two or more individuals. Here are some pointers:

- Maintain eye contact with all of those interviewing you.
- Acknowledge each person by their name and shake each of their hands.
- Involve everyone in the conversation, even though one person may be asking the questions and the others are merely observing.
- Build rapport and connect with everyone. One of the advantages of a panel interview is that you have the opportunity to impress more than one person. Their decision to select a candidate for the job may be reached by majority vote or by adding up their scores on each candidate and choosing the highest score. The more likeable you are to the individuals on the panel, the more likely you will get the majority vote or a high score.

Interviews at Job Fairs & Networking Events

Although job interviews are commonly held at a company's site, interviews can also occur at job fairs. These present a more social, casual, and less intimidating environment. For example, some job fairs in Las Vegas, Nevada, are held in banquet or convention rooms in a hotel. What is becoming even more popular is the fusion of a job fair and a networking event.

During a job fair, an employer that conducts on-the-spot interviews may have set aside a space in which to conduct their interviews or you may have to interview in public. As discussed previously, you may be interviewed simultaneously with other job seekers or in front of a panel. If an employer does conduct on-the-spot interviews, you will most likely be meeting with some of the staff from the company's HR department.

Here are some pointers to consider:

- Offering alcohol is a great strategy if you are the recruiter interviewing at that event. It can be a trap for those interviewing. You may think that you are able to hold your liquor, but you may not always be aware of what you are saying or even doing. This type of environment may help you relax, but you can get too relaxed, put your guard down and start rambling on and on and "spilling the beans." This, of course, can be a bad thing since you may be divulging more information than necessary.
- It may also be a test to determine how responsible you are. If you drink at the event and plan on driving home afterwards, employers may wonder whether you can responsibly weigh the risks and outcomes of your decisions. My recommendation is to avoid the alcohol and keep a clear head.
- Remember, this event is meant for you to connect with employers, not to pick up a date. Because it's in a casual setting, like a restaurant or someplace with a bar, you are free to mingle with employers as well as with other job seekers. It's ok to mingle and make small talk with others. If

you do meet someone you would like to meet again, set a separate time to have that meeting. Remember, you are there to connect with employers. Stay focused and keep relationships with employers professional. It is an inappropriate time for you to ask an attendee out on a date.

Here are some suggested books for further information in the area of communication:

Effective Comunication in the Workplace: A Pratical Guide to Improve Interpersoanl Communicaiton in the Workplace for Better Environment, Client Relationships, and Employee Engagement by David L. Lewis

How to Say It: Choice Words, Phrases, Sentences, and Paragraphs for Every Situation by Rosalie Maggio

The Art of Body Talk, How to Decode Gestures, Mannerisms, and Other Non-Verbal Messages by Gregory Hartley and Maryann Karinch

The Definitive Book of Body Language by Allan and Barbara Pease

10 Skills for Effective Business Communication: Practical Strategies from the World's Greatest Leaders by Jessica Higgins, JD, MBA, BB

CHAPTER 3.

INTERPERSONAL COMMUNICATION SKILLS

"No matter what your line of work is, even if it is in either one of the technical professions, your degree of success depends on your ability to interact effectively with other people." -Dale Carnegie

Work Well with Others:
Diversity & Adaptability in the Workplace

Understanding others will help you interact, communicate, and work better with people from different backgrounds, which may include ethnicity, culture, religion, age, sexual orientation, values, or even personality. You must be able to work in teams, communicate with all levels of management and employees, and be able to fit in with the organization. Organizations vary in size, values, structure, culture, and even philosophies. You must assess the level of organizational fit you have with a prospective company and how much you are willing to compromise:

- Are your skills valued in this organization?
- Is the size of the organization suitable for you?
- Are the values of the organization in alignment with your values?

Your Personality for the Job & the Workplace

In 2016, I was invited to an HR open house at the Palms Casino Resort Hotel in Las Vegas, NV, a property owned by Station Casinos as of this writing. They invited HR professionals and workforce representatives to learn about their hiring and screening process so that we could more efficiently refer qualified candidates. They told us that they intentionally have all the interviewees wait in a room until each is called into their interview; however, they told us that the interview actually started when the candidates walked into the waiting room. The hiring managers and HR staff would observe how each candidate interacted with one another. For example, if they saw a candidate for a bartender position not being friendly and engaging with others, they made their decision not to hire that person even before speaking with them. Being friendly and engaging are important traits to have as a bartender. Once you are on company property, be aware that people may be observing you and act accordingly.

Richard Branson wrote and published an article on LinkedIn in September 23, 2013, titled, "How I Hire: Focus on Personality." In the article, Branson said, "There is nothing more important for a business than hiring the right team. If you get the perfect mix of people working for your company, you have a far greater chance of success." He went on to say, "The first thing to look for when searching for a great employee is somebody with a personality that fits with your company culture. Most skills can be learned, but it is difficult to train people on their personality. If you can find people who are fun, friendly, caring and love helping others, you are on to a winner. Personality is the key." (1)

Intro to Behavioral Styles and Personality Types

There are various studies on and models of behavioral styles and personality types. In this chapter, I will briefly mention a couple of them. You may have already been exposed to some behavioral styles and personality tests during a company assessment or questionnaire when you submitted your online job application. Regardless of whatever personality types you may be familiar with, this book introduces you to the concept that the attributes of your behavioral styles and personality type relate to your work performance, your communication style and your interpersonal relationships.

Results from various personality assessments can vary. How these models and types are derived comes from years and years of research and debate; thus, these are more complex than can briefly be explained in this book. I provide short explanations in this book to provide a basic understanding of personality, and more importantly, to understand how it applies to acing your job interview. Because these personality assessment models are complex and each can be explained in a book all on its own, I have provided the titles of some further reading at the end of this section if you want to dive deeper into the subject. You should use these and a variety of other sources and methods as a guide in deciding the kind of person you are, want to be, and the type of work that you enjoy in doing.

There are some stark differences between personality types. Each have their strengths and weaknesses and should not be used as a predictor of success or failure. For example, one can argue that you should be more outspoken and outgoing to be successful. However, some well-known, public figures, or so called "successful people" are actually soft spoken and are known to be quiet people, such as Mark Zuckerberg, Tony Hsieh, and Abraham Lincoln. While not a predictor of success, learning your personality type and the personality types of others will help you better communicate, interact, and work with others. Learning about the similarities and differences between you and others helps you formulate an approach when building rapport, collaborating, working together, and even when trying to influence someone to hire you.

DISC Assessment

DISC is a behavior-assessment tool based on the theory of psychologist William Moulton Marston that centers on four different personality traits. This theory was then developed into a behavioral assessment tool by industrial psychologist Walter Vernon Clarke. DISC is the acronym for:

D -Director/Driver, Dominance

- Bold, direct, blunt, and to the point.
- Competitive and ambitious. Likes challenges and even confrontations.
- Takes charge and is quick to delegate but impatient when giving instructions.
- Impatient, especially if you are not moving as quickly as they think you should be.
- Insensitive to others' feelings. Lacks diplomacy or tactfulness.

I -Influencer/Socializer, Expressive
- Possesses the gift of gab: very sociable, loves talking, and can talk a lot.
- Great at persuading, selling, and promoting.
- Optimistic, inspirational, and creative.
- Impulsive: tends to leap before they look and buys things based on emotion.
- Dislikes paying attention to detail, repetitiveness, and rework.

S -Supporter/Amiable-Relator, Sympathetic
- Friendly and sensitive to other people's feelings.
- Great listeners and very sympathetic.
- A great team player: great at coordinating and cooperating with others.
- Wants harmony and unity: looks for ways to get everyone involved.
- Dislikes confrontations: tends to go along with things even when they disagree.

C -Conscientious Thinker/Technical, Analytical
- Detail-oriented: likes to be accurate, precise, organized, and efficient.
- Great at problem solving, organizing, planning, and creating systems.
- Dislikes working in unpredictable or disorganized environments.
- Prefers to work alone to get work done based on his or her quality standards.
- Can be overly analytical and suffer from "paralysis by analysis." (2)

Your DISC Profile

Aligning yourself with a job based on certain behavioral styles can help you select the job that is best suited for you. Your behavioral style is important to know can be useful in deciding on whether a job suits you or not. For example, if you are a C -Conscientious Thinker, your attention to detail is an essential trait for a job that requires you to be meticulous and accurate.

You likely have some characteristics from each of the four behavioral/personality types. The sequential order of those characteristics, from most dominant to least dominant, creates your DISC Profile. For example, a DISC Profile could be: CSID or ISCD. There are numerous websites and books where you can learn more about DISC and even take an assessment to discover your DISC profile.

The Holland Codes (RIASEC)

The Holland Codes or the Holland Occupational Themes, known by the acronym RIASEC, is the theory that careers should be based upon personality. It was initially developed by American psychologist John L. Holland. RIASEC is the acronym for:

R: Realistic (Doers)

- Likes to work with things requiring physical labor, motor skills, or strength.
- Interests tend to focus around the scientific or mechanical rather than cultural or aesthetic areas.

- Action oriented and prefers to use realistic approaches to solve problems rather than thinking about them and using abstract theories.

I: Investigative (Thinkers)
- Likes to observe and conduct research to understand information.
- Prefers to work independently rather than interacting with people.

A: Artistic (Creators)
- Creative, inventive, and likes to work with ideas.
- Challenges rules and structure.
- Open to opinions and different perspectives.

S: Social (Helpers)
- Likes to work with people and finds satisfaction in helping others.
- Prefers to work with people rather than working with data.

E: Enterprising (Persuaders)
- Likes to work with people and data.
- Prefers one-on-one relationships to build rapport, trust, and influence.
- Tends to be a good talker and skillful in persuading others.

C: Conventional (Organizers)
- Likes to work with data and information rather than interpersonal situations.
- Likes to approach things in a more structured way using well thought out methods rather than

winging it or approaching it with unstructured methods and theories.

- Likes rules and regulations that are clear, rather than unclear rules with grey areas. (3)

These six personality types are categorized and arranged on a hexagon. You tend to primarily resemble one personality type but may also have aspects of one or more of the adjacent types on the hexagon. Conversely, you will likely have little in common with the personality type on the opposite side of the hexagon. The order in which you identify with each of the six types is your personality pattern. Thus, Holland's RIASEC hexagon model suggests 720 possible personality patterns. (3)

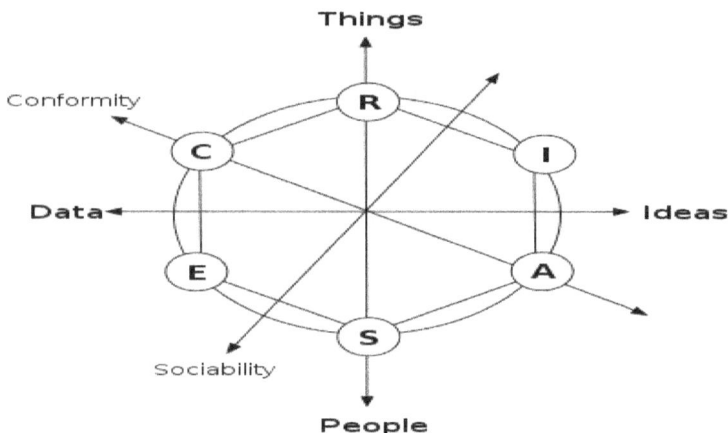

Picture of Holland's RIASEC hexagon model obtained from Wikipedia. (3)

The Holland Codes suggest that people will be more successful and satisfied working in an area that compliments their personality. Matching yourself to a job based on your personality can also help select the type of job or career that may be best for you. For example, if you are an Investigative type of person who prefers to conduct research over persuading people, doing market research for a company will likely be more satisfying and comfortable for you than selling the company's products or services.

While Wikipedia shows an example list of careers in each personality type, there are other numerous websites and books where you can learn more about the Holland Codes and even take an assessment to discover your personality type and do some career exploration.

Myers-Briggs (MBTI)
The Myers–Briggs Type Indicator (MBTI) is an introspective self-report questionnaire indicating differing psychological preferences based on how people perceive the world and make decisions. It is based on 8 characteristics, 4 continuum pairs of opposing traits:

Extroversion I – (I) Introversion
The first continuum is about how a person processes information:
- Extraverts prefer to think and process new information with other people rather than on their own.
- Introverts prefer to think and process new information on their own rather than processing it with other people.

Sensing (S) – (N) Intuition
The second continuum is about what people focus their attention on:
- Sensing types are good at understanding things that are tangible but have a difficult time understanding abstract things and ideas. They prefer learning things when they are presented in a detailed and organized manner.
- Intuitive types are good at understanding abstract things and ideas. They prefer learning things they can relate to or that are insightful or meaningful to them.

Thinking (T) – (F) Feeling
The third continuum is about a person's decision preferences:
- Thinking types prefer to make decisions using logical principles and reasoning.
- Feeling types prefer to make decisions based on gut feeling and consider other people's motives.

Judging (J) – (P) Perception
The fourth continuum is about how a person handles complexity:
- Judging types tend to have a structured way to approach things. They always try to integrate new information into their structured approach. They are usually inflexible to change.
- Perceiving types tend to be unstructured and keep options open. They are more flexible to change and can improvise without having a prior structured approach. (5)

The resulting personality score will look like a set of 4 letters from each pair, such as ESTJ or ISFP or ENFP. The underlying assumption of the MBTI is that you all have specific preferences in the way you perceive experiences, and these preferences underlie your interests, needs, values, and motivation. (5)

Note: New concepts have been gradually added. **MBTI Step II** is an extended version of the Myers–Briggs Type Indicator. Step II provides additional depth and clarification within each of the four original MBTI preference pairs. (5)

There are numerous websites and books that explain more about Myers–Briggs Type Indicators and even offer an assessment.

People Skills

In the workplace, employees want to work with people they like, respect, trust, and who are team players. So, whether you realize it or not, your social skills will be tested in a job interview. Your people skills will be on display whenever you interact with the interviewer or other company employees, such as the security guard, the front desk representative, one of the staff that passes by you or shares an elevator with you. Make sure that you are pleasant to everyone.

Some people prefer working alone, but there is no way around dealing with people. No matter what position you fill, you will always be interacting with people. You will at least need to interact with other employees and managers, if not customers. If you are an introvert, it's ok; just learn the personalities of others so you can interact with them when necessary. As discussed earlier, you do not have to be an extrovert to be successful. Each personality type has its own strengths and weaknesses and is not a predictor of success or failure.

In a job interview, interviewers can gauge how well you work and interact with others by asking questions such as:
- Describe a time when you worked in a team?
- Tell me about a time you had a disagreement with a previous supervisor or coworker and how you handled it?
- Describe a time when you received constructive feedback from your previous supervisor or coworker?

- Describe a time when you dealt with a difficult customer or a customer complaint.

Build Rapport & Make a Connection
"Connecting is the ability to identify with and relate to people in such a way that it increases your influence with them." -John C. Maxwell

Rapport is key in building mutual trust and respect. You can also influence another person once you build rapport. You prefer to do business with people you know and like. Some job candidates fail to realize this going into the job interview. Remember, as previously discussed, how personality plays a major role in hiring decisions? You may have all the skills and experience for the job, but if you come across as being an ass to people, no one will want to work with you. Why would anyone hire you if you will likely create animosity in the workplace?

There may be some time for "chit chat" or "small talk", even in an interview. Use every opportunity you get to build rapport and make a connection.

Here are some suggestions to build rapport and connect:
- Find common interests you have with the person, the company, and the people you will be working with. Discuss some of these common interests briefly and see if you can weave in how you can add value to the company. Caution: be mindful about discussing personal matters. Refer to "Discussing Employer's Concerns" and "Sharing Too Much Information" in Chapter 1.

- Address people by their names during your discussions. It makes you seem more personable and can help you remember their names, which may leave a lasting impression with them.
- Genuinely listen. Make them feel important and that you respect them.
- Communicate and relate at their level. Refer to "Mirroring" in this chapter.
- Be mindful not to make inappropriate jokes or any negative comments or connotations.

Building Rapport with Humor
The appropriate use of humor allows you to:
- Make your message more memorable,
- Appear friendly and accepting,
- Gain attention,
- Relieve tension,
- Enhance relationships,
- Increase trust, and
- Distract or divert the discussion from a negative topic.

Use humor cautiously, especially in a job interview. Get a feel for who you are talking to before going for it. It is preferable to avoid jokes, at least in the early stages of the interview process. You may not know the interviewer well enough yet and may misinterpret their personality. Also, avoid discussing or joking about politics and religion. Your jokes may be perceived as inappropriate or even offensive.

Mirroring & Neuro-Linguistic Programming

In neuro-linguistic programming, also known as NLP, you do or say something that will psychologically get the other person to like you, agree with you, or do something you'd like them to. You may have used neuro-linguistic programming in your life without even realizing it or knowing what it is called. For example, you pick up a piece of chocolate cake and put it in front of your friend who is trying to resist the temptation to take a bite. You say to your friend, "Come on, just take one bite. You know you want to." With those actions and comments, you are programming your friend to take a bite of that cake.

Some strategies discussed in this book can be incorporated into your neuro-linguistic programming: dressing for success; giving a firm, professional handshake; researching the company for information to discuss in the interview; and even delivering an impressive value proposition when you are asked the question, "Why should we hire you?"

Mirroring is a popular method of neuro-linguistic programming. It entails copying a person's mannerisms to build rapport and make a connection. Note: you should not mirror everything. For example, if the interviewer has an accent, only use the accent if you truly have the same accent, otherwise you may be perceived as mocking them.

In Chapter 2, we discussed verbal, vocal, and visual methods of communication. You can incorporate your neuro-linguistic programming strategies, like mirroring, into your communication. You can mirror or use:

- Body language, postures, and gestures;
- Facial expressions, eye contact, and emotions;
- Volume and pace of voice, including pauses, breathing, and non-verbal sounds;
- A handshake when first meeting the person and when leaving the meeting;
- Comfort Zone/Personal Space: the distance you maintain from others;
- Words, including languages and references both of you are familiar with or buzz words to gets them enthusiastic or hyped up about something; and
- A discussion about a subject the both of you share an interest in, such as a similar sport or a similar hobby.

Here are some suggested resources for further information in the area of interpersonal communication and people skills:

Article: "How I Hire: Focus on Personality" by Richard Branson.

Book: <u>Dealing with People You Can't Stand: How to Bring Out the Best in People at Their Worst</u> by Dr. Rick Brinkman and Dr. Rick Kirschner

Book: <u>Do What You Are: Discover the Perfect Career for You Through the Secrets of Personality Type</u> by Paul D. Tieger

Book: <u>How to Win Friends and Influence People</u> by Dale Carnegie

Book: <u>Quiet: The Power of Introverts in a World That Can't Stop Talking</u> by Susan Cain

Book: <u>The Four People Types: And What Drives Them</u> by Steven Sisle

Book: <u>Type Talk at Work: How the 16 Personality Types Determine your Success on the Job</u> by Otto Kroeger

Book: <u>Wired That Way: A Comprehensive Guide to Understanding and Maximizing your Personality Type</u> by Marita Littauer

Book: <u>50 Best Jobs for Your Personality</u> by Laurence Shatkin, Ph.D.

Website: Onetonline.org
Onetonline.org is free website sponsored by the U.S. Department of Labor, Employment & Training Administration, and developed by the National Center for O*NET Development. It has a link to the *O*NET Interest Profiler*, a self-assessment tool that you can take to help you explore your interests, how your interests relate to the workplace, and what kind of careers might be best suited for you.

Here is the link to the *O*NET Interest Profiler*:

https://www.mynextmove.org/explore/ip (4)

CHAPTER 4.

SELLING SKILLS

"You need to buy what you sell if you are going to have true integrity. You need to believe in what you do. Have a passion for what you do where you just love what you do. You need to believe that your services will be good for them." -Tom Hopkins, Mastering the Art of Selling

You Must Believe in Yourself Before You Can Sell Yourself

To sell yourself effectively, you must first believe in yourself. It is difficult to persuade someone to believe in you if you have a difficult time believing in yourself. I could never feel confident in selling cigarettes because I don't smoke and don't believe in cigarettes. Which could you confidently sell, a product you have used for years and years or a product you dislike and have never used? When you are applying for jobs, you are the product you are selling to an employer. Be confident in selling yourself by believing in what you are selling.

Some people may feel uncomfortable in sales, while others seem to have a natural ability selling to others. Regardless of how you feel about sales, everyone has selling skills and you need to use them to ace any job interview. Everyone recognizes that you're selling if you are trying to influence someone to buy a product or agree with you on an idea or service. But you also are selling when you are trying to convince someone to hire you or when you are trying to obtain a promotion.

As discussed in Chapter 1, concerns about what the interviewer thinks about you may cause you to start questioning yourself, creating self-doubt. This, in turn, can lead you to lose confidence in your abilities. While it's important to be honest with yourself and recognize your weaknesses, it's also important to identify how you can turn your weaknesses into strengths so that you can sell those strengths as benefits to employers. Building your self-confidence starts with believing in yourself. Believing in yourself makes selling yourself a lot easier and will help you make a compelling sales presentation. Trust the process.

"You need to believe that your services will be good for them. People will say yes more to your belief, your conviction, than they will to your technical skills." -Tom Hopkins

Integrity & Honesty in Selling

Some of us may have felt suckered into buying something from a salesperson and later developed buyer's remorse. Maybe you discovered that what was said and promised by the salesperson was not true. Or maybe the features or benefits of the product were not as expected. There are those people in sales who sell things they don't believe in, who "fake" their way through a sale or even lie. Faking and lying just to make a sale doesn't end well for either the buyer or the seller. The buyer gets buyer's remorse and does not do business with that salesperson again. He may tell a friend about the experience and word of mouth may spread like wildfire, ruining the reputation of the salesperson, as well as the product and the company involved. This example is not meant to bad mouth the sales profession, but as in any profession, there are some "bad apples" in the bunch.

To determine your integrity level, the interviewer may probe deeper into a subject to determine whether what you say is true. It only makes matters worse if you go on lying confidently throughout the interview. If you are caught in a lie by the interviewer, everything you say thereafter becomes questionable. They wonder what else you are lying about. Being dishonest will not only disqualify you from the job but can also tarnish your reputation and credibility.

The best way to prove you are honest is to deliver on your promises. To do otherwise brings anything you have said and your professional values into question. If you are at a job interview, however, it can be difficult to prove your honesty to someone you've just met. Here are some strategies to help demonstrate your honesty and integrity:

- Keep your first promise by showing up to the interview on time.

- Give examples of your past work experiences and achievements when you demonstrated honesty, integrity, and delivering on your promises.

- Provide testimonials and letters of recommendation from references: those people who worked with you or observed your work, such as coworkers, managers, supervisors, and even clients, who can vouch for your character.

Although the best strategy is to be honest, you will need to be careful how much information you divulge. You learned how to address some employer concerns in Chapter 1. Remember to always present yourself in a positive light. There are some preferred words you can use from the sales business to sell yourself in a positive way while still telling the truth. For example: If you have a spotty work history and worked at several retail stores each for only a short period of time, instead of mentioning that, you can better sell yourself in a more positive light by saying something to the effect, "I have been in the retail industry for over five years so I have an in-depth knowledge of all aspects of the business, from distribution to sales and everything in between."
Integrity and honesty are also covered further in Chapter 12.

Needs Analysis

Find ways you can add value to the company to demonstrate how beneficial it would be to hire you. To do so, you will first need to find out what the company's needs are.

Conducting Your Market Research: Gathering Information About the Company
If the company offers shares of stock to the public, the shares of stock are likely traded on a stock market, such as the New York Stock Exchange, Standard & Poor (S&P) 500, or the Nasdaq. Publicly held companies are required by law to disclose and make available their financial reports. These quarterly and annual reports are especially helpful for shareholders and investors. They are also an excellent source of information for you when researching the company. They can tell you:

- The progress of the company's short-term and long-term goals.
- The managerial approach and the way of operating and doing business.
- The challenges, setbacks, and problem areas of the company.
- The company's financial health, including any possible layoffs or expansions.

You can research a company's financial reports on their website, usually found on the Investor or Investor Relations Page. You can also find a company's financial reports on the U.S. Securities and Exchange Commission's (SEC) website on their "Search Company" page.
https://www.sec.gov/edgar/searchedgar/companysearch.html (1)

If the company is not publicly traded, it is not required to disclose financial reports to the public. Here are some other ways to learn more about a private company:

- Review the company's marketing and advertising materials, such as its website, social media page, brochures, radio and television commercials, and even business cards. You can find a wealth of information from such sources, like what products and services they offer, their mission statement and values, their business philosophy, names of the mangers at the executive level, etc.
- Review the marketing and advertising materials of the company's competitors. They can tell you something about the industry, their market share, etc.
- Visit the Better Business Bureau's website at bbb.org. It may provide you with some information regarding the company, especially if there have been reports and complaints about the company's business practices.
- Review website job boards, such as Glass Door for more information about the company and possibly some reviews from other job candidates who have posted and shared their job interview experience.
- Speak with current employees of the company. They can provide insight into the daily work environment. Pay attention to what they say about the company culture, about how employees are treated, etc. Some job seekers try to be discrete when interviewing employees. I think it is best to seek approval from HR before speaking to employees. Not only does this keep everything aboveboard but it also demonstrates

how interested you are in the position. You may also develop relationships that can lead to internal recommendations.

Understanding the Organization's Culture and Values

Diversity, personality, tolerance, values, customs, rituals, and traditions are some of the things that define an organization's culture.

You can learn about a company's culture by doing research on the company. Prior to the interview, you can pay the company a visit, even ask for a tour. You may be given the opportunity to talk to and interview employees of the company. If you already know someone in the company, that's even better; you can get the "inside scoop" from that person.

At your interview, be aware of your surroundings. Observe your physical surroundings: the layout and décor of the offices; posters and frames on the walls; the way people greet and interact with each other in the break room, hallways, and in their offices; what is being talked about on bulletin boards, etc. Just observing these minor things can give you an idea of whether the company encourages camaraderie, team building, growth and development in the workplace. Are people being recognized for their achievements? Perhaps there are pictures of employees being recognized for meeting or exceeding sales quota for the quarter or being recognized as employee of the month. Is the company involved with the local community? Perhaps they offer employees time to volunteer at local nonprofit organizations. Does the company allow people to decorate their offices? Are there family pictures on employee's desks? Are their calendars filled with deadlines?

Your observations are important for building rapport and connections with the people at the company, especially the interviewer. Find ways to show how you fit in with the company's culture and work environment. Your observations will also play an important role in how you answer some of the interview questions.

Gathering Information About the Interviewer

Researching the company and the job position can be a lot easier than researching the interviewers. Some companies publish press releases, which may give you an idea of the type of people who work for the company. If you know someone on the inside, they may be able to clue you in. Here are some other ideas of where to look to research interviewers:

- Review the company's website, social media, press releases, newsletters, and any other company publications that may mention their employees' bios, promotional announcements, etc.
- Read up on key personnel's profiles through LinkedIn (A professional social media site where you can connect with other professionals.) If you don't know the interviewer, it may be best to introduce yourself by messaging the person first before asking to connect with them on the site. If you know someone from the company, ask them to refer you to others in their network.

- Interview employees and former employees of the company.
- Interview those who have done business with the company.

Here are some of the people you may meet in the organization during the interview process:

- ### Human Resource Personnel
Recruiters for the company can also be part of the company's HR department. These individuals oversee the recruiting, screening, and hiring process. They also verify the information on your job application, conduct criminal background checks and reference checks.

- ### Hiring Manager
This individual will likely be your potential immediate supervisor, so he or she will most likely measure your abilities to ensure you can perform the job duties.

- ### Employees and Staff
These people will likely be your potential coworkers, so they will most likely measure how you get along with others and whether you would fit in with the company.

- ### Business Associates
These individuals are the internal customers of a company or business partners of the company. They may serve as interviewers in order to measure how you deal with customers, including dealing with customer complaints and problems.

- *Small Business Owner*

This individual is the owner of a business, who may play some or all of the roles mentioned above. Here are some things to consider when interviewing with a small business:

- A small business may not have an HR department or staff, so the business owner may be doing his or her own interviewing and hiring. He or she may not be well-trained or knowledgeable in all aspect of human resources, including employment and labor laws. When dealing with a business owner, do not challenge his or her intelligence; however, if you come across a question or something in a job interview that is inappropriate or illegal, be assertive and point that out.
- Some small businesses may not have an employee handbook or written operating procedures, so if you are hired ensure you understand and have the following in writing: how work performance will be evaluated, absentee guidelines, advancement and promotion opportunities, pay structure, etc. Ensure you understand any contracts and paperwork that you sign.
- A small business can also be a family business where nepotism may exist so procedures and policies may favor family members over outsiders.
- Some small businesses may hire a third-party company to conduct their preliminary selection process or may hire a staffing company to obtain temp workers or temp-to-hire workers.

Understanding the Interviewer
Do your research so you understand how your interviewer thinks and how he or she makes hiring decisions. This will be advantageous because you will know how to approach and sell yourself to them. If you've previously owned or operated a business with employees, you most likely understand the concept of hiring the right candidate for the job. This concept of selecting the right candidate for the job is no different than selecting the right childcare center to place your child in, or the right contractor to remodel your home, or even the right mechanic to repair your car. You do your due diligence rather than hiring someone at random. Employers do their due diligence, as well. They screen job applicants to find those best suited for the job. Thus, part of your focus in a job interview is to convince the interviewer that you are the best candidate.

Once you have gathered all the information, including any suggestions or advice from others, you need to draw your own conclusions and decide how to approach the job interview, how to deliver your elevator pitch, and how to answer the interview questions.

In the book, You Have 3 Minutes!, written by Ricardo R. Bellino founder of Trump Realty Brazil, on pages 69 and 70, Bellino explains how he was able to deliver an effective three-minute pitch resulting in a deal between him and Donald Trump. Some people thought his idea to get Donald Trump to buy into an idea of Villa Trump in Brazil was a long shot. Trump gave Bellino a window of opportunity of only 3 minutes to personally meet with him and convince to approve the idea. Before presenting his idea to Donald Trump, he presented to numerous consultants. They all strongly advised that he eliminate most of his marketing ideas and focus on the numbers because they believed Donald Trump was most interested in the potential money to be earned. Bellino understood that the numbers were important; however, he also understood that Donald Trump was also about marketing. He recognized that "The Donald" likes to promote, if not brag, about his brand, his image, his reputation, his business ventures, and his successes. If he hadn't recognized that important piece of information, he would have taken the advice from the consultants and may not have closed the deal. (2)

Bellino also suggested that I include some valuable advice from Donald Trump's book Think Like a Billionaire. Trump said, "Ricardo Bellino had exactly three minutes to give me his business presentation. I was extremely busy that day and not particularly in the mood for a presentation, so I thought he might decline, which would free up my day a bit. Not only did he not decline, he gave me such a great presentation within those three minutes that we became partners. It's surprising what people can do with a deadline. I mention that because sometimes we have to give ourselves deadlines. Practice giving your presentation in under five minutes. Practice giving your introduction in less than three minutes. You will discover that you can be an effective editor by cutting out everything that isn't absolutely necessary. Your audience, or your superiors, will be grateful for your ability to distill the essence for them." (3)(2)

You Are a Sales Professional

In a job interview, you are conducting a sales presentation, so behave as a professional:

- Be on time for the interview. Be considerate. You were given a window of opportunity. Seize the moment.
- Dress appropriately for the interview.
- Bring a resume, a professional portfolio, and/or other essential materials required to sell yourself in an interview.
- Present yourself with a positive attitude and with confidence.
- Offer a handshake to the people you meet and when you are leaving.
- Be sincere and genuine in your performance. Interviewers can spot a phony act. Present an honest view of yourself that matches your personality.

Your Value Proposition

Some people may call this an elevator speech. Hey, whatever works for you. I call it a value proposition to remind you to mention something of value you have to offer to the employer. Most people tend to emphasize how great they are for the job but fall short when delivering the message that they are who the employer needs and wants. The key to delivering an effective value proposition is to point out specifically what it is you bring to the table. Read carefully through the job posting and the job description so that you know exactly what the employer needs and wants. Then craft your value proposition based thereon. You can use the "I have, I can, I am" method as a guide.

"I Have.., I Can..., I Am..." is a simple tool that can help you structure and remember what you should mention in your value proposition. You have anywhere from 30 seconds to just a few minutes to impress the employer, so make those few seconds or minutes count.

I Have...
is a statement of your significant achievements.
- "I have over 5 years of HR/Recruiting experience."
- "I have a Master's Degree in Business."

I Can...
is a statement of your abilities.
- "I can use ATS software to determine a job match for each job applicant."
- "I can type 65 words per minute."

I Am...
is a statement of identity.
- "I am detail oriented and excellent at reading and evaluating people to determine whether they are a match for a certain position."
- "I am a self-starter who takes initiative and likes to take on new challenges."

Closing Value Proposition Statement
This is where you remind the interviewer that you have what they need and want.

Give them a glimpse of yourself that will be memorable. Perhaps give an analogy, compare yourself to something similar highlighting a relevant trait. For example, "I am like a Shih Tzu, outgoing and friendly; working here in the animal shelter, the animals need someone like me who cares and can be their friend, as well."

Mention how your background will help you push the company forward. For example, "As the Sales Manager, my 10+ years of sales experience and proven track record of increasing sales by 30% will allow me to lead your sales staff in not only meeting expectations but beating them."

Other Guidelines to Consider in Your Value Proposition
Your approach for delivering your value proposition will also be guided by the position you are interviewing for and the company you are interviewing with.

You may need to take a more aggressive approach for a sales position and a more conservative approach for other types of positions. For example, in sales, there is usually a call to action at the end of a sales presentation. If you are in a job interview for a sales position, an aggressive approach to your call-to-action strategy could be to have the interviewer make an on-the-spot decision to hire you. "I am a sales professional who is a go-getter. One of my strengths is closing and I always work to pursue a yes from my clients and not leave until I get one. Are there areas of concerns I can clarify for you so that you feel comfortable in making the decision to hire me now?"

Selling & Storytelling

You can showcase some of your abilities, such as time management and interpersonal skills, in the way that you present yourself in the job interview: from the time you arrive and how you dress to how you interact with people in the organization.

There will be other times when you will need to showcase your abilities by articulating your thoughts, giving examples, and storytelling.

You will need to organize your thoughts and ideas to be able to speak coherently and clearly present your skills, abilities, and qualifications in a story. Articulating your thoughts and ideas is one of the necessary skills you will need to work on mastering to make your job interview a success.

The SAR Method: Situation-Action-Result

Interviewers ask questions to which you must respond with an elaborate overview of your abilities and how you handle certain situations and problems.

One of the most effective methods to prove to an employer that you have the attributes they are looking for is to answer the question by telling a story or giving a descriptive example. You want them to be able to visualize how you applied your skills and abilities to solve a difficult problem or deal successfully with a task.

Situation: Explain to the interviewer the situation and who or what was involved.

Action: Explain the action that you took and why you chose that action over other alternatives. Also, explain what resources you needed to gather in order to execute your plan of action.

Results: Explain the results or the outcome of your actions, including if expectations were met, if the problem or issue was resolved successfully, or if the action you took was unsuccessful and what you learned from that experience.

For example, one of the ways to explain your customer-service skills and experience is to walk through a complete sale, including your thought process and the highs and lows of the deal. Explain how you dealt with the customer's complaint, solving the customer's problem, or even how you assisted a customer in making a purchasing decision.

By telling a story or giving a specific example, you can convey your
- Goal planning and project management skills,
- Multi-tasking and coordinating skills,
- Can-do attitude and work ethic,
- Relationship- and team-building skills, and
- Conflict-resolution and problem-solving skills.

When you develop your stories and examples, ensure to:
- Incorporate the attributes that the company is looking for;
- Communicate how valuable you are;
- Explain in detail how you dealt with a certain problem;
- Highlight your most significant contributions;
- Share something you succeeded in that was extraordinary or against the odds;
- Point out any recognition or awards you received for your performance; and
- Describe how you earned those accomplishments or achievements.

Other key points to consider:
- Your stories should be relevant and important for the interviewer to know.
- Keep your stories brief. Structure your stories to last from 2 to 5 minutes. You do not want to drag on and on so that the interviewer gets bored and loses attention.
- Be prepared for any follow-up questions.

Keep Adding Value

Provide Extraordinary Service & Sell Yourself as "Extra-Ordinary"
Telling a story about your everyday work routine does not get an employer excited about you. What sets you apart from the rest of the candidates? How can you add value to the company? Find ways that you can be helpful to the company; maybe offer ideas to improve efficiencies or incorporate a story of a time you went above and beyond. You need to sell yourself as an "Extra-Ordinary" person who will add value to the company.

Be wary of highlighting additional skills you have outside of the job description. If they will be hiring you as a business analyst, avoid including the skills of an IT along with your business analyst experience even though you may have some IT background and work experience. Everything changes, including salary and responsibilities, if they expect you to be both a business analyst and an IT. At the interview, one of the interviewer's jobs is to explain the responsibilities and duties the position entails. Your job is to convince the potential employer why you are worth a certain amount of pay for the position you seek. Refer to Chapter 7 for more information on negotiating skills.

Provide Solutions
Display your problem-solving and leadership qualities by offering possible solutions to company-specific or industry-wide problems, even at the interview. Show that you genuinely want to help the company succeed.

- When researching the company, gather information on what problems the company is currently facing or look for potential problems the company may soon face. At the job interview, share your findings and offer some solutions.
- At the interview, ask the interviewer to identify some problems the department or company is facing and offer some solutions. Explain how you will go about solving the problem.
- At the interview, you can also offer to volunteer to lead a team or a project and explain how you will go about solving the problem.

Demonstrate respect and invite constructive feedback. Be mindful of the way you convey your message when offering your solutions to the company's problems. Offering to make radical changes when you are not even hired yet can make you seem arrogant and cocky. You also do not want to embarrass the employees who have suggested or tried other methods.

Highlight Your Record of Success to Impress
Taking pride in your historically progressive accolade of achievements and successes and believing yourself to be the best adds even more to your value proposition. At the job interview, demonstrate your confidence and discuss some of your achievements and successes. The more relevant or relatable your successes are to the job you are seeking, the better. If you never had a job before or you are just getting back in the workforce, the key is being able to translate previous accomplishments into relevant successes. You must demonstrate that you are looking to progress and strive for excellence.

Using Visual Aids
In Your Interview Sales Presentation

You should walk into a job interview prepared, preferably with a visual aid to enhance your interview sales presentation.

Your presentation can include:
- Diplomas & School Transcripts,
- Certifications,
- Achievement Awards & Recognitions,
- Letters of Recommendations & Referral Letters
- Work Samples (Drawings, Paintings, Pictures, Photographs, etc.), and/or
- A PowerPoint presentation (depending on the job you apply for).

You most likely will not need to prepare a PowerPoint presentation for an entry-level position but I would suggest you have at least a professional portfolio ready. Include samples of your work if you are a Writer, Photographer, Model, Graphic Designer, Painter, or even an Auto-Detailing Technician.

A demonstration video may also be needed if you are applying for on-screen positions, such as News Reporter or Professional Entertainer.

Remember, these marketing materials should not be the only means you have to sell yourself. To get hired, you must continuously build rapport with the interviewer, deliver your value proposition, and conduct yourself in an interview with professionalism. Sell yourself!

In this book, I place Referral Letters in a different category than Letters of Recommendation. A Referral Letter is similar to a Letter of Recommendation, but I classify them differently because they come from two distinct types of sources. A regular Letter of Recommendation could be written by your previous supervisor or employer. A Referral Letter comes from your contact within the company or from someone else who has a close relationship to an employee of the organization. A Referral Letter could be written by your previous supervisor who is now currently with the company you are applying for. A Referral Letter could also be written by someone in a Staffing Agency who is referring qualified candidates to the company. A Referral Letter is a powerful tool that can influence a hiring manager's decision to hire you. If you have an employee of the company who is willing to put their reputation on the line to recommend you, that speaks volumes. Hence, networking is the key to getting a Referral. There is some truth to the saying, "It's not what you know, it's who you know."

Things to Discuss at the Interview

Although you cannot plan every minute of an interview, here are some guidelines to help keep the conversation flowing:

- Don't let your resume do the talking for you at the interview. Further elaborate on the work experience listed on your resume.
- Bring a professional portfolio that includes your certifications, samples of your work, awards and achievements, and Letters of Recommendation for further discussion.
- Approach the interview as if you were a consultant for the company. Add value from the start rather than waiting until after you're hired to add value.
- Do research on the company and the people you will be meeting with. It will help you formulate questions and allow you to demonstrate that you have done your homework. Taking the time to do your homework demonstrates a good work ethic, strong interest in the company, and respect for the interviewer.
- Find out who you will be meeting in the interview and research them so that you can find common ground to build rapport.
- Pay attention to the time. Be considerate of the interviewer's time. If you think you have not yet made a strong impression, work to continue the conversation to give yourself the opportunity to redeem yourself. Make it worthwhile for the interviewer to continue the conversation.
- When asked whether you have any questions, use this opportunity to continue the conversation

with the interviewer. Refer to "Sell Yourself by Asking Questions", "Selling and Storytelling", and "Keep Adding Value" in this chapter for more ideas on what to discuss.

Things You Should Avoid Discussing at the Interview

Here are some guidelines for avoiding certain topics in an interview:

- Avoid discussing topics that may convey that you are more interested in how you can benefit from working at the company rather than how the company can benefit from hiring you. Avoid discussing things like compensation and benefits. You do not want to convey the message that compensation and benefits are more important in your job selection than adding value to the company.
- Avoid discussing any personal relationships with your references. You may be best friends with the interviewer's coworker or a referral but what you do outside of work is irrelevant in a job interview.
- Avoid discussing personal topics, issues, or problems such as childcare, transportation to and from work, or relationship problems. Also avoid creating a negative mood. Refer to "Positive Attitude, Positive Environment" in Chapter 1.
- Avoid discussing or making a joke about divisive topics, such as religion and politics.
- Refer to "Questions You Should Not Ask" in this chapter for more ideas on what not to discuss.

Sell Yourself by Asking Questions

Asking questions shows that you are interested in the job and the company. Use this opportunity to continue to sell yourself. You take control of the conversation by asking questions. Ask questions that lead the discussion to a certain topic, such as

Qualifications for the job
- What would I need to accomplish for you to tell me that I have done an outstanding job during the first ninety days?
- What do you think are some of the major challenges for this position?
- Can you tell me what a typical day would be like for this position?
- Do you feel my skills and experience align with what you are looking for?

Company culture
- What do you like most about working here?
- How would you score the company on living up to its core values?
- Where do you see the company in three years and how would someone in this position contribute to its success?
- How would you describe the company culture?

Advancements and growth potential in the company
- What is the company doing to support professional development?
- What is your staff turnover rate and what is the company doing to reduce it?
- What is one of the most interesting projects that you have worked on?

- How does the company measure progress in the department?

Leadership style within the company
- What are some of the problems your company is currently dealing with and what is the company doing about it?
- How do you handle conflicts between your staff members?
- How do you evaluate success here?
- Who will I be working most closely with and what is their management style?

The hiring process
- What is the next step in the interview process?
- Is there anything else I can provide you with to help you make your decision?
- Is there anyone else you would like me to meet?

I think you get the point by now. Refer to "Things to Discuss at the Interview", previously covered in this chapter.

Questions You Should Not Ask

You should not ask questions that make you seem more interested in what's in it for you than what's in it for the company. Here are some examples of questions you should not ask:
- What is the salary?
- When and how long are breaks and lunch breaks?
- When can I take a vacation?

You should keep the conversation focused on what value you can bring to the company. Sell yourself by highlighting the skills you bring and how you can add value to the company.

The Art of the Close

While it is customary for interviewers to end the interview by saying you will be contacted if you are selected to move forward in the hiring process, you should strategize how to end the interview on your terms. Because you are conducting a sales presentation when interviewing, you should also have a close to your sales presentation. There are many closing strategies you can use, as a closing in sales is more of an art than it is a science. Tailor your closing sales presentation to the job you are applying for.

If you weren't asked if you have any questions yet, incorporate asking questions into your close. Remember, if you have not gotten the offer yet, you should attempt to continue the conversation until they say yes. By asking questions, you take control of the conversation.

No matter what other strategies you use, remember to incorporate some type of call-to-action strategy. In a sales presentation, there is a call to action to get the other person to say yes and buy the product or service. In your call to action, you may need to take a more aggressive approach for a sales position and a more conservative approach for other positions. For example, if you are in a job interview for a sales position, your aggressive call-to-action strategy could be to have the interviewer make an on-the-spot decision to hire you. "I am a sales professional who is a go-getter. One of my strengths is closing and I always work to pursue a yes from my clients and not leave until I get one. Are there areas of concerns I can clarify for you so that you feel comfortable in making the decision to hire me now?" For other positions, demanding the job may seem pushy and rude.

In sales, if the person does not end up buying your product or service, you request a follow-up appointment. Use this same sales strategy in a job interview. If you were not given a job offer at the end of the interview, do not leave the interview without setting a time to follow up. You will need to approach your request to follow up in a subtle way so that you do not come across as pushy or demanding. Also, do not come across as being too arrogant, cocky, or overly confident by saying something like, "Thank you for your time. I enjoyed being able to discuss where I can add value to your company. Call me to let me know when you would like me to start." You should say something like, "Thank you for your time. I enjoyed being able to discuss where I can add value to your company. When would be the best time for me to follow up on this opportunity to be a part of your company? Would next Tuesday at 10:00 am be ok or would 3:00 pm be better for you?"

The Follow-Up

After the job interview you need to continue to market and sell yourself.

You should send a letter of appreciation to the interviewer and everyone else you met at the job interview, including the person who referred you for the job. The letter should
- Show your appreciation for their taking the time to discuss with you the opportunity to learn more about the position and the company.
- Highlight certain areas that were discussed at the interview and what you learned from the interview.
- Mention your experience with each person you met, the way they treated you, and what you liked about them.
- And of course, continue to mention your qualifications and the value you can add to the company.

You should also conduct a follow-up call or send a follow-up letter to stay in the forefront of the interviewer's mind.
- You should have different variations for each follow-up message. If you keep sending the same letter or keep saying the same thing over and over, that can get boring and annoying.
- Your message should be brief. The recipient of your message may not have time to read a "novel" or may not have the time to speak to you over the phone for 20 minutes.

You can send your message via email, "snail" mail, LinkedIn, or any other media platform where you think it will most likely get attention and be read.

Should you stop by the office to follow up?
Common business etiquette is to arrange an appointment rather than to show up unannounced. Showing up unannounced can be considered rude, even in business, which does not leave a good impression of you. If you do get the ok to stop by the office, ask who you will be meeting with. Perhaps you will be meeting with a senior executive of the company who may be the decision maker. Prepare to go to the meeting as if you have another interview even if you weren't told it's going to be an interview. Remember, when you are onsite, you are on stage. Always make a good impression.

How often should you follow up?
Most employers are not obligated to contact every job candidate with an update. You should follow up rather than waiting for a call, which you may never get. The frequency with which to follow up has been debated among job candidates as well as employers. Too frequently can make you seem desperate and can be annoying. Too infrequently can make you seem uninterested. So, how much is too much? Well, you should at least conduct one follow-up call. Then send a follow-up letter about a week or so after the call. If you still do not get a definite response, send a letter of appreciation. That is already a total of three follow ups. If there is still no response, you need to decide whether to continue to follow up or move on to pursue other

opportunities. If you are applying for a sales position, however, especially one that requires "hard selling," it may be a test of your persistence, so it may be wise to continue to follow up.

Evaluate Your Interview

Right after the interview, you should write down your experience and take notes while your memory is still fresh. Write down in detail what you remember from the interaction. Be as detailed as you can.

Here are some questions to ask yourself and some guidelines for evaluating your interview

- Evaluate your experience. Most interviewers will not usually spend time after the interview to go over what they liked about you, what they disliked about you, or what they thought about how you dressed. You will have to assess yourself.

- What were the questions asked? What were your answers? How did you answer the questions? Were you able to deliver the message you wanted to convey? What was the interviewer's reaction to each of your answers? If you are applying for similar jobs at different companies, there is a high probability that you will be asked similar questions when you interview at those companies. These are the questions you should prepare for.

- What topic or skill did the interviewer emphasize during the interview? Some interviewers emphasize certain traits they are looking for in a candidate and will hint several times during the interview to see if the job candidate mentions that he or she has that particular trait. For example, when the interviewer emphasized that they are looking for someone who is a team player, did you show the interviewer you are a team player through your storytelling examples?

- When you assess yourself, be honest but don't beat yourself up over it. Allow yourself to accept your own constructive criticism. You have no control over the decision at this point and all you can do is evaluate, learn from your experience, look at areas where you can improve, and move forward. There may be times when you know the interview went well and, yet, you do not get the position. It happens.

Learning More about Selling

One of the best ways to learn sales techniques is to learn from successful sales professionals. Watch how they conduct their sales presentations, handle objections, conduct negotiations, and make their closing statements. You can also read up on sales practices or attend seminars and workshops. However, to get better at selling, you must sell. There is no way around it. Remember, selling is a life skill. Everyday find opportunities where you can apply and practice the sales techniques you learned. The more you sell, the more you will feel comfortable selling.

Here are some suggested books for further reading in the area of selling:

How to Master the Art of Selling by Tom Hopkins

Selling 101: What Every Successful Sales Professional Needs to Know by Zig Ziglar

Small Message, Big Impact. The Elevator Speech Effect by Terri L. Sjodin

The Little Red Book of Selling by Jeffrey Gitomer

The Psychology of Selling by Brian Tracy

You Have 3 Minutes! by Ricardo R. Bellino

CHAPTER 5.

IMPROMPTU SPEAKING SKILLS

"Impromptu is more of an art form of communication than it is a science." -Robert Ritua

Have you ever watched comedians like Chris Rock. Paula Poundstone, Gabriel Iglesias, Ellen DeGeneres, or Jeff Dunham, who improvise some of their material while on stage? They are talented comedians who can have a conversation with someone in the audience, unrehearsed, and come up with a joke from that conversation on the fly. You do not need to be that good, but definitely take some time to develop your impromptu speaking skills.

Job interviews are not an everyday experience, so when you do have a job interview you tend to rehearse your elevator speech and answers to typical interview questions.   Although it is important to rehearse, it is nearly impossible to memorize every answer to every possible job interview question.   Thus, the need to exercise your impromptu speaking skills. Some people think impromptu discussion or improvisation is just "winging it." But improvising is actually skill that needs to be practiced in order to excel at it. You should never go to a job interview unprepared and try to "wing it." You should consistently exercise and apply your skills and abilities so that you are as prepared as possible for the interview. Being adaptable is covered in Chapter 9 and critical, creative, and quick-thinking skills are covered further in Chapter 10.

To develop my communication skills, I joined a Toastmasters club. Toastmasters International is a nonprofit, educational, and global organization that teaches public speaking and leadership skills. In a typical Toastmasters' meeting there is usually a segment for Table Topics, a portion of the meeting where the Table Topics Master will present a question and will call upon a member at random to answer the question, like a pop quiz. The members do not know the questions ahead of time and do not know if they will be called upon to answer one of the questions; thus, they do not have time to prepare an answer. The member called upon to answer must think quickly and deliver a brief impromptu, unplanned speech. It's a great opportunity to develop impromptu speaking skills. You can visit the Toastmasters' website at Toastmasters.org to learn more and to visit a club near you.

As covered in Chapter 2, learn to read the interviewer's reactions so that you can modify your responses, or even the direction of the conversation, based on how they respond. When improvising, you must gather information and pick up clues to get a feel for the interviewer and where the conversation is going and should go. You and the interviewer can alternate in leading the conversation. In Chapter 4, I discussed asking questions as a way to lead the discussion towards a specific topic. Also, note which topics are discussed in more detail than others. Learn to recognize what the interviewer is trying to emphasize in those discussions. Explore what, specifically, the interviewer is looking for.

What if things do not go as you expect? What if a question takes you by surprise? What if you make a mistake or say something accidentally embarrassing? Unforeseen circumstances can occur in the workplace so you should also expect unforeseen circumstances to occur in a job interview. Always expect the unexpected. Learn to improvise and move on with the conversation.

In an improv class, students learn several exercises to improve their quick-thinking, improvisational skills. One of the exercises is the call-back strategy. Call back is basically recalling something that was mentioned in the conversation to:

- Emphasize or bring up a certain point or topic;
- Get clarification of something that was mentioned; or
- Revisit a certain topic, perhaps to add to or to retract what was said.

When you must give an impromptu response, you can use call back to slow the conversation down. For example, repeat or rephrase what was said or what the interview asked you. You can use this strategy to stall for time while you gather your thoughts into an intelligent response.

In improv, you also learn to keep the conversation moving. You avoid saying "No" or saying something negative that may stop the conversation from moving forward. Learn to accept whatever is said and add "Yes, and..." to keep the conversation moving forward. For example, even though you may not agree with the interviewer, you should avoid saying, "No, I don't agree with you." Instead, you should say something like, "Yes,

I understand your point, and I would also like to mention that..." This strategy keeps the conversation in a positive light, avoids tension, and welcomes constructive criticism and different perspectives.

Although you want to move forward with the conversation, be careful not to give too much information. Giving too much information can work against you. You should give just enough information to paint a picture. Keep the information relevant to your message. However, make sure not to leave out important and relevant information. Keep the theme of the conversation focused on meeting the employer's needs rather than your own. For you to convince the interviewer that you are the right person for the job, you should gently weave the threads of your responses into how you meet the employer's requirements.

Put Your Skills on Autopilot

"The knowledge and skills you have achieved are meant to be forgotten so you can float comfortably in emptiness, without obstruction." -Bruce Lee

Just because you need to improvise in a job interview does not mean you should go in unprepared. Rehearsing allows you to offer your value proposition in a strategic way and helps prepare you for conversations in an interview.

Even though you want to create meaningful conversation, always have some topics in mind to discuss in order to keep the conversation flowing and relevant in an interview.

In Chapter 10, we discuss critical, creative, and quick thinking in more detail.

Improving your analytical and creative thinking along with setting the intention to have a meaningful conversation will allow you to be in the moment and improvise when necessary, without worrying what to say next or how to answer the questions. You can present your authentic professional self rather than come across as a scripted professional. Remember, the interviewer needs to be able to visualize you fitting in with the company. If you are perceived as too scripted, you may come across as fake instead of genuine and sincere. Companies don't want a phony in the workplace. They want someone who is genuine.

At the job interview, these skills should run on autopilot. It's like learning a self-defense technique. When you first learn a certain technique, you start off slow in your training, taking it step by step. Next, you gradually learn to apply it with an opponent when sparring. When the time comes for you to apply that technique in a real life-or-death situation, you automatically execute the technique without thinking about it. You should train yourself the same way for any job interview.

Too often I see people put a lot of pressure on themselves and they tend to tense up and create more stress for themselves. I understand a job interview is important for you and nervousness can set in but, putting a lot of pressure on yourself can hinder you from performing your best at the interview. You can be so focused on your concerns that you can't prepare properly for the interview. You may start asking yourself: What if I don't get the job? What if I mess up at the job interview?

You should rehearse for a job interview until it becomes second nature. Meditation and applying positive self-talk can also help. You should practice the skills mentioned in this book on a daily basis to have it work on autopilot in the interview. Doing these things will help alleviate some of that stress and pressure. You should be going into the job interview with a clear mind and focused on the task at hand.

Here are some suggested books for further reading in impromptu speaking:

Ditch the Pitch, The Art of Improvised Persuasion by Steve Yastrow

Magic of Impromptu Speaking: Create a Speech That Will Be Remembered for Years in Under 30 Seconds by Andrii Sedniev

CHAPTER 6.

MARKETING SKILLS

"A brand for a company is like a reputation for a person. You earn a reputation by trying to do hard things well." -Jeff Bezos

A company uses branding as a method of creating a distinct image or reputation. Your personal branding is your professional image: what people perceive about you based on their experience with you or what they have observed, read, or heard about you.

Your Brand Message

1. Your brand message must emphasize that you have what an employer is looking for. It must also address these areas of concern:
   - Besides having the minimum qualifications, what else can you offer and contribute to the company?
   - What do you have that makes you valuable to the company?
   - What sets you apart from the rest of the candidates?
2. Be aware of how you are marketing and branding yourself in social media. You can be judged by how you portray yourself or by how you are being portrayed in a public forum.

3. Your strengths, professional values, work ethic, skills, personality, and professionalism must be integrated in your brand message.

Your SWOT Analysis

You may be familiar with the SWOT analysis in marketing. Businesses use SWOT Analysis to solve problems and develop strategies, especially for marketing. You can use SWOT Analysis, as well, since you are marketing yourself to employers. You can analyze your strengths and weaknesses and think about what opportunities and threats exists due to those strengths and weaknesses. Below is an example of a SWOT Analysis. See if you can answer #3 in each of the categories.

STRENGTHS	WEAKNESSES
1. Possess a high school diploma	1. Not very proficient in math
2. Likes working with and talking to people	2. Does not do well with confrontations
3.	3.

OPPORTUNITIES	THREATS
1. Able to apply for jobs that require a high school diploma	1. May not do well in jobs that require using a lot of math
2. Enjoys jobs that require interacting with people most of the time	2. May have difficult time dealing with customer complaints
3.	3.

First Impressions
Through Your Marketing Materials

Although this book focuses on skills and strategies you can apply to ace any job interview, it is important to point out that your first impression starts from the moment that you apply. Recruiters and potential employers are reading your resume and cover letter and checking your online profile, including your social media, blogs and comments, and any news articles about you. You can develop a certain reputation based on how you market and promote yourself.

First Impressions Through Your Referrals

An introduction by a referral can help market you and influence an employer's decision. An employer can more easily learn about you even before you personally meet them face to face. In fact, a referral's introduction of you could be why you received a job interview in the first place. However, if you do not live up to the expectations the referral set for you, the referral and the employer can feel disappointed and maybe even deceived. This situation can be difficult to reverse, as your tarnished reputation precedes you. Furthermore, you also tarnished the referral's reputation. The referral may feel embarrassed, fooled, and become an unhelpful source. Why would this referral refer you for another job opportunity ever again?

First Impressions Through Your Wardrobe

"Dress like you own the bank, not like you need a loan from it." -Adil Laresh

Some people like to express themselves by the way they dress. The way they dress makes them unique. There is a time and a place to stand out; most times, an interview is not one of them.

The way you dress in a job interview affects how an interviewer perceives you. Impressions matter a lot. You may have heard this several times and I don't want to make it sound like I am beating a dead horse; however, it's important to emphasize dressing appropriately because there are still plenty of candidates who walk into an interview inappropriately dressed. It may be common sense, but do not walk into a job interview under- or over-dressed.

When going to a job interview for an executive or senior-management position, you don't necessarily need to wear an Armani suit, just as you don't necessarily need to wear scrubs for a medical position. However, you should still walk into the job interview in professional business attire.

So, what does it mean to dress in professional business attire?
What is appropriate to wear in a job interview?
A more appropriate question to ask is:
How does the company define professional business attire and business casual attire?

Finding out the company's dress code policy and culture is one of the reasons why it is important to do your research. It may be necessary to visit the company prior to the job interview just to scope things out. You don't have to go in as a secret shopper; you can be honest and tell them you have a job interview in a few days and would like the opportunity to learn more about the company. You can request a tour. Some companies may already offer tours of their facility or you may be introduced to their public relations department. You can observe how people are dressed and get an idea of the company culture. Is the company lax on the dress code in the workplace? Is it a tight-knit type of community? How do they treat guests and customers? Were there people being interviewed during your visit and, if there were, how were they dressed?

Many businesses apply psychological concepts into their marketing. Grocery stores place fruits and vegetables at the front of the store rather than the back because colors invite customers to enter. The smell of popcorn as you pass by the concession stand to go to the movie theater makes you crave it. Lights continuously flashing on slot machines in a casino attract attention and entice guests to play. It can up your chances to make a good first impression if you also apply some psychological concepts in your job interview. For example, colors can evoke an emotion and can help you convey a certain message. Wearing a blue tie can help convey confidence and trustworthiness. Wearing a red tie can help convey being confident and assertive. What these colors convey are subjective but, use any opportunity you have, no matter how small you think it is, to sell yourself, including applying some color

ACE THE JOB INTERVIEW   AceTheJobInterview.Win

schemes in your wardrobe when going to a job interview. To see how you feel and what you think when you see these colors, try this exercise: look at the color tie the Presidents of the United States wore when they delivered a speech. Do you feel the color of the tie they wore helped give meaning to the message they delivered?   Does it seem they strategically used a certain color tie for a specific speech?

Wearing a black, blue, gray, or brown suit is a more traditional, if not conservative approach, when going to a job interview. Wearing colors such as green, yellow, orange, or purple can be considered too flashy. You want to create a good first impression and leave the interview being remembered in a positive way.

Paying attention to detail also applies to what you wear. Even the little things can make a big impact in creating a certain impression. The color and design of your tie. The watch that you wear or the eyeglasses you may be wearing. The piece of jewelry dangling from your ear or from your nose. The tattoo on your forearm or on your neck. The color of your hair or your purse.

Page 125

Here are some suggested books to learn more about marketing and branding:

Knock 'em Dead: Social Networking: For Job Search and Professional Success by Martin Yate

Platform: Get Noticed in a Noisy World by Michael Hyatt

Use Social Media to Find Your Dream Job! How to Use LinkedIn, Google+, Facebook, Twitter and Other Social Media in Your Job Search by Dan Quillen and Dr. Lance Farr

CHAPTER 7.

NEGOTIATING

"My salary situation at 'Morning Joe' wasn't right. I made five attempts to fix it, then realized I'd made the same mistake every time: I apologized for asking." –
Mika Brzezinski

As discussed in Chapter 4, everyone uses their selling skills both in their personal and professional life. Similarly, everyone also uses their negotiating skills with their family, friends and business associates. If you have kids, you negotiate with them, so they finish their homework, do their chores, or eat their vegetables. If you are at work, you negotiate with your coworkers to trade assignments or negotiate with your supervisor to create better a work schedule.

There may be times when you need to negotiate with an interviewer, especially when it comes to salary. You can also apply negotiating tactics at the end of an interview or when meeting a recruiter at a job fair. Maybe you are told to contact the company's HR department to follow up with your application. You may need to apply negotiating and sales tactics to get the contact information of the decision maker. With some finesse, you may be able to obtain the information.

The dialogue and duration of the conversation will depend on your and the interviewer's skill and experience in salary negotiations. Here are some guidelines:

Conduct your research before going into the job interview. You should already know the salary range for the position and some of the fringe benefits the company offers prior to the interview.

In a job interview, be patient. You should not be the first person to bring up salary. The discussions about salary usually occur in follow-up interviews rather than in the initial interview. Do not discuss salary if you have not received a definite job offer. And even then, wait until they initiate the conversation on salary.

If you can, you should actually lead the discussion away from the discussion of salary. Even if the interviewer provides a starting amount or quotes a salary, regardless if you agree with the amount or not, continue to discuss your qualifications and how much value you can bring to the company to prove to the interviewer your worth. Refer to "Things to Discuss in an Interview" in Chapter 4 for suggestions on what topics to bring up and discuss. You can lead the discussion away from salary by saying something like:

- "I appreciate you bringing up salary, but my previous position entailed different responsibilities and I would like the opportunity to further discuss the differences. How do you see me bringing value to the company based on our conversation so far?"
- "I still have questions about my responsibilities before you talk about salary. Could I first ask you about _____?"
- "I enjoy working in this type of environment and I feel I can add value to your company. Until a

decision has been made to definitively hire me, I think discussing salary is premature. If it's ok with you, I would like to share with you some of my other qualifications in detail first."

So, When Do You Discuss Salary?

Negotiating is more of an art form than it is a science. You will need to rely on your instincts as well as good judgement to determine when it is time to discuss salary.

Times when you should discuss salary:

- When you are definitely hired and are ready to negotiate compensation.
- When the interviewer feels that you have the qualifications and can add value to the company and he or she has said you are definitely hired.
- When you understand what the job entails, are compatible with the company's culture, values, and policies, and are comfortable with what the company has to offer.

When the discussion of salary starts, avoid being the first to name an amount.

Companies have their own pay scale for each position based on the job market, which allows for some flexibility when negotiating a salary with a prospective employee. So, you may not be able to directly compare what you were earning at your previous job to an offer from another company.

The salary you are offered is usually what the company thinks the position is worth based on supply and demand in the job market. If there a lot of openings for a particular job but a low number of qualified job applicants, the salary for that particular position is usually at the high end of the pay scale. If there are a lot of job applicants applying for a particular position, the salary is usually at the lower end of the pay scale.

Prior to the interview, research the company, the salary for the position, any benefits, and even the current and local job market so you can go into the job interview with a salary range in mind. Have a low limit and a high limit. If the interviewer insists on getting a desired salary from you, you could say, "Based on the responsibilities this job entails, it is reasonable the pay would be somewhere from $35,000 to $45,000. Is that consistent with your expectations?"

When the interviewer does insist on getting a desired salary from you, you need to use your best judgement on whether to further discuss salary after providing your desired salary range. Keep in mind the general rule of thumb: avoid having a conversation about salary if you have not received a job offer. Strategize your discussions. If you need to, refer back to what was previously covered in this chapter for what to say to lead the discussion away from salary.

Getting an Offer

When you get an offer, keep calm and don't rush to make a decision. If it is lower than expected, you should continue to discuss your qualifications and how much value you can bring to the company to prove to the interviewer you're worth the salary you asked for. Also, remember there may be other aspects of the offer that you may be able to negotiate to compensate for a lower salary, such as:

- Future raises and bonuses,
- Health & Dental Insurance/Group discount rate,
- Life & Disability Insurance/Group discount rate,
- Personal leave/Personal days off,
- Vacation and sick leave,
- Tuition reimbursements/assistance,
- Childcare center/assistance,
- Flextime work schedule,
- Profit sharing and stock options, and/or
- Travel reimbursements.

Put it in Writing

Ensure what was agreed upon is in writing, usually in a letter of agreement or employment contract. Having a contractual agreement:

- Ensures what was agreed upon is documented.
- Ensures there is no ambiguity and both parties understand what was agreed upon.
- Ensures the agreement specifically explains the terms and conditions of employment, including compensation, any fringe benefits, and conditions of termination.

Here are some suggested books to learn more about negotiating:

How to Negotiate a Killer Job Offer: The Job "Secret Agent" Series by Robin F. Bond Esq.

How to Negotiate at the Workplace: Emotion, language, how to ask for a raise, negotiating your salary, negotiating vacation time, job interview negotiation tactics (Negotiations at the workplace) by Brian Fortune

The Art of Negotiation: Life is all about negotiation. Learn how to win in life by learning how to close a deal! by Peter Oliver

CHAPTER 8.

BUSINESS ETIQUETTE

"Business etiquette is the behavior and manners considered appropriate in the business and professional world. Business etiquette involves rules of conduct that allow us to communicate with people in business and to interact with them in a civilized manner." -Lillian Hunt Chaney and Jeanette St. Clair Martin, The Essential Guide to Business Etiquette (1)

The majority of the topics in this book, such as branding yourself by the way you dress and conducting a sales presentation in an interview, are categorized under communication skills. It is important to point out, here, that business etiquette is just another aspect of communication. There are certain professional manners, demeanors, and forms of communication expected in the workplace.

You use business etiquette whenever and however you communicate with the employer, whether it's phone calls leading up to the interview or follow-up emails afterwards.

Use what you learn from your research to figure out how to conduct yourself with the people from the company.
- Learn all you can about the company and the people in the organization.
- Learn about the company's mission, vision, values, culture, etc.

- Find out the hierarchy of the organization: Who's the President or CEO of the company; the managers in each department, particularly in the department you will most likely be working in; and who will be interviewing you. You don't want to go into the job interview without at least knowing their names.

Here are some business etiquette concerns you may have:

What if you are introduced to various people in the company or if there are multiple interviewers? You should offer a handshake and greet each person you meet. Remember as you initiate the handshake, make direct eye contact, introduce yourself, and smile.

Greeting everyone you meet in the company is a great way to make a good first impression in an interview. Shake hands and express a pleasantry. When you meet with the interviewer, start by shaking his or her hand and extend a greeting, "Hi, I am Robert Ritua. Thank you for setting aside time from your busy schedule to discuss career opportunities with me." The interviewer may continue with some pleasantries. Incorporate your skills into the discussions whenever possible, even during pleasantries. For example, if asked if you had problems finding the place, you can say, "There was construction on a road a couple of blocks away, so I had to take a detour. Luckily, I drove by the area yesterday to make sure I could find this place." This shows you are responsible, can manage your time, plan well, like to be prepared, and that you are taking the job interview seriously.

What if you are offered something to drink?
Some people are more receptive and are easier to communicate with when they are relaxed so employers may offer you something to drink to get you to relax and, perhaps, let your guard down. To be safe, politely say no thank you. Some employers may even have a hidden agenda when offering you something to drink, especially if offering an alcoholic beverage. You definitely should say no in that instance.

Should you sit or stand in an interview?
Regardless if there are chairs to sit in, always wait until the interviewer welcomes you to be seated. If the interviewer takes a seat and does not offer you one, ask politely if you can sit down. Some interviews may be conducted while standing.

What about using profanity?
Reality check: some people do use profane language even in the workplace. When I was in the Navy, it was considered a norm for people to swear and curse. However, there is always a time and place to use profanity and the job interview is not it. Even if the interviewer or someone you meet at the company uses profanity, you should not mirror this behavior. Mirroring and building rapport were discussed in Chapter 3. However, you can still build rapport without using profanity. In a job interview, always display professionalism.

More Business Etiquette Tips
In a job interview, you may be asked:
- How would you explain to a long-time business customer that their services are no longer needed?
- How would you approach an employee who has been with the company for over 10 years to tell them that he or she must be let go?
- Why is business etiquette important in the workplace?

In some interviews, you may need to take a test where you must apply business etiquette when writing or typing a
- Business letter,
- Email correspondence, or
- Report or briefing.

You may also be asked to demonstrate business etiquette by
- Conducting a presentation
- Auditioning or role playing
- Delivering a speech
- Giving an oral report
- Completing an assigned task or some type of simulation

Guideline for maintaining professionalism throughout.
- Keep calm and level-headed.
- Speak with confidence and conviction.
- Maintain eye contact.
- Use appropriate body language. A handshake at the beginning and end of the interview. Sit up

straight or, if standing, stand erect. No slouching. No facial expressions of disgust and/or frustration. Hand gestures should complement your communication.

- Listen and pay attention. Don't just listen with your ears. Listen using your other senses as well, such as interpreting the interviewers' body language, facial expressions, and gestures. Also, pay attention to your surroundings. Your surroundings may give you clues that can help you in an interview.
- Be engaging. Observe the 50-50 rule in communication. Although the ratio may not be exact, mix speaking and listening 50-50 in the interview.
- Maintain positivity. Never say anything negative about anyone or any business.
- Never divulge too much personal information such as marital status, family status, car problems, etc.

Here are some suggested books to learn more about business etiquette:

Global Business Etiquette: A Guide to International Communication and Customs by Jeanette S. Martin and Lillian H. Chaney

The Essential Guide to Business Etiquette by Lillian Hunt Chaney and Jeanette St. Clair Martin

The Power of Nice: How to Conquer the Business World with Kindness by Linda Kaplan Thaler and Robin Koval

PART 2

OTHER IMPORTANT PROFESSIONAL VALUES & SOFT SKILLS

"Your core values are the deeply held beliefs that authentically describe your soul." -John C. Maxwell

Communication is paramount to your success, so it was covered extensively in Part 1. Part 2 will cover other professional values/soft skills needed to ace any job interview. There are many soft skills that are important and Part 2 only mentions some of them. While it is impossible to talk about all the soft skills in detail in this book, I mention those that I think are core soft skills necessary to incorporate in any job interview. If you find other soft skills that you deem necessary to apply in a job interview, you can incorporate them in your daily practice to enhance those skills, as well. As I have emphasized many times in this book, it is more important to enhance the soft skills that you already have than to focus on memorizing answers to potential interview questions if you want to ace a job interview.

CHAPTER 9.

DEPENDABLE, ADAPTABLE, COACHABLE, TEAM PLAYER

"I can't change the direction of the wind, but I can adjust my sails to always reach my destination." -
Jimmy Dean

Dependable

In the workplace, being dependable is not just about showing up to work on time and doing your job. It includes completing tasks on time, as promised. It includes following instructions, taking on more responsibilities, and staying until the job is done. It includes being trusted and staying ethical when difficult situations arise. It includes maintaining your cool when you are dealing with a difficult customer. It even includes providing quality work and giving your 110% attention and focus on any job task that you do, even when your supervisor or coworkers are not watching. Employers look to see if a candidate can be entrusted with their money, supplies, trade secrets, products, and even their brand reputation. Will you work in the company's best interest? If you held a previous job, an employer may wonder why you want to work for a different company. Do you lack loyalty?

Or, if you are still in school, will your schedule be flexible? Employers expect you to show up to work on time and not have any problems with tardiness and absenteeism. Employers should not be the one to lecture you and train you on these basic life skills. Employers expect you to police yourself. You must have the ability to follow instructions and manage your own work and responsibilities. Submitting your application before the deadline, showing up to the interview on time, and preparing for the interview by having your resume and list of professional references ready, are some examples of being dependable.

Dependability encompasses all the other professional values. In a job interview, give more examples of how you can be depended upon. You should mention previous work experience or an achievement that demonstrates dependability. You must demonstrate that you are a self-starter, someone who takes the initiative, and someone who is a fast learner and can be trusted to follow instructions and work with minimal supervision. You must also demonstrate that you can plan and organize your responsibilities, which includes prioritizing your tasks, setting goals, implementing plans to meet those goals, and monitoring and evaluating your progress and results.

Adaptable

Being adaptable in the workplace can take many forms. It could be that you are flexible in your work schedule, thus able to work any shift you are scheduled for. Maybe there will be a situation where you will need to adjust your normal daily routine due to an unexpected event, such as temporary computer system shutdown. Someone may call in sick and you may need to take on extra work that day. There are many possible scenarios in which you will need to improvise and think and act quickly on your feet. There may be even situations on the job where you will need to perform duties outside your job description. You need to be adaptable.

You must also demonstrate that you can integrate your skills, personality, and values into the company with minimal time and training. Improvisation was discussed in Part 1 and being able to think quickly on your feet is discussed in this part of the book. Refer back to those sections for more information on adaptability.

In a job interview, even with preparation, there may be surprises. You may be asked unexpected questions. Be calm and answer those questions confidently and enthusiastically to the best of your ability. Avoid displaying uncertainty and doubts. Being level and cool-headed in unforeseen situations shows employers you are adaptable.

Coachable

Some people may not take instructions well, especially when they are given by someone younger or with less work experience. Years of experience do not translate to being coachable. For example, if you have been driving for many years, you may consider yourself an experienced driver. Do you remember when you first learned to drive, where you had to position your hands? Did you place your hands at the ten o' clock and 2 o' clock positions? Where are your hand positions when you drive now? Be honest. Do you continue to drive with your hands at the ten o' clock and 2 o' clock positions or do you drive with one hand? With years of driving, you tend to develop bad habits. The same concept holds true with work experience. If you are set in your own ways, an employer may think it is too much trouble to retrain you. Demonstrate that you are coachable.

Team Player

Becoming a great team player is crucial. It involves collaborating and learning to get along with others who have different points of view. It also includes the ability to give and take constructive criticism, holding each team member accountable, and giving credit where credit is due. Employers like to see someone who can be depended upon to do their part. In a job interview, convince an employer you are a team player by giving specific examples of how you worked well with others. For example, mention a team project you worked on and what role you played in its success.

Showcase Your Professional Values

Here are some interview questions you may be asked to determine the extent of your dependability, adaptability, and ability to work in a team:
Why do you want to work here?
What is your dream job?
Why do you want to work and represent our company?
Explain a time you went above and beyond.
Tell me about a time you took on new assignments?

Tell me how long it took you to learn something new on the job?

When giving a story, highlight the use of your skills and professional values. For example, when I was in the Navy assigned to Patrol Squadron Nine, stationed at Kaneohe Bay Marine Corps Base Hawaii, there was a strong windstorm sometime in 2002 or 2003. Because the hangar was old, I'm guessing it was probably built sometime before World War Two, the windstorm caused damage to the roof. When it rained, water leaked through the entire building so that it seemed like it was raining inside, too. Until the roof could be repaired, electrical power could not be turned on in the hangar. Instead of stopping operations, we adjusted how we did business. We all learned to be resourceful and adaptable. We utilized portable power generators to power up essential computers and other office equipment so we could continue our day-to-day operations. We had buckets placed everywhere inside the building to catch the water that would seep through the roof. We began to appreciate the sun more, relying heavily on sunlight while working outside the hangar during the day so that the night shift had power for the lanterns and flashlights they needed. We borrowed the other squadrons' hangars when a plane needed major repairs since the other hangars didn't sustain as much damage as ours did. We worked under those conditions for about a week until the roof was repaired enough so that the power could be turned back on. We didn't give up or complain, we did the most we could with what we had and learned to conserve our resources. That is the kind of story that will showcase how adaptable and coachable you are while also highlighting that you are a team player.

Here are some suggested books to learn more about soft skills:

Do Improvise: Less Push. More Pause. Better Results. A New Approach to Work and Life by Robert Poynton

Soft Skills That Make or Break Your Success: 12 Soft skills to master self, get along with, and lead others successfully by Dr. Assegid W. Habtewold

The Hard Truth About Soft Skills: Workplace Lessons Smart People Wish They'd Learned Sooner by Peggy Klaus

The 55 Soft Skills That Guide Employee and Organizational Success by Dr. Tobin Porterfield & Bob Graham

10 Things Employers Expect Their Employees to Know: A Soft Skills Training Workbook by Frederick H. Wentz

CHAPTER 10.

CRITICAL, CREATIVE, & QUICK THINKING

"I love it when a plan comes together." -John "Hannibal" Smith, The A-Team

Have you ever watched classic TV shows of the 1980s, such as the A-Team or MacGyver? In both of those shows, the main characters often find themselves in predicaments where they must improvise by using whatever is available to them at that moment to create a contraption to either escape or set a trap to capture the bad guys.

When I was in the Navy assigned to Patrol Squadron Forty-Seven between 1994 and 1999, one of the commanding officers had a pet peeve: an individual complaining about a policy of the organization without suggesting how to fix it. He would say, "If you are going to present a complaint, it helps if you can provide us with a solution." His philosophy may seem to relieve management of the responsibility for solving a problem, but in reality, it empowers the individual to solve problems and not feel helpless. You do not have to hold a management title to come up with great ideas to solve even some of the most difficult and complex problems of the company. Besides, getting input from people within the organization increases workplace morale because employees feel they can contribute to solutions and make change. Some companies even reward and recognize individuals who save them money with their creative solutions.

Using Your Critical-Thinking Skills
to Solve Problems

Critical-thinking and problem-solving skills are not just for managers. Critical thinking allows you to methodically, rationally, and logically think through the challenges and problems you face in your life and in the workplace, especially when under pressure and in stressful situations. You will be much more valuable to an employer if you are the go-to person who can be relied upon to handle and resolve problems. The key is to be able to explain to an employer the process you took to come up with a solution to a problem. You must also be able to demonstrate the process you used to analyze and strategize while solving the problem.

How Wild Are Your Ideas
and How Imaginative Your Creativity?

You may not think that you need creative skills because you are not applying for a job as an Artist, Graphic Designer or Architect; however, you will need to use creative skills throughout your job search and interviews. These traits complement your ability to improvise and think quickly on your feet. Selling, promoting, and branding yourself will inherently involve applying creative skills and imagination. You will need to come up with a way to stand out from the rest of the job candidates and be memorable.

Whether you go conservative or take the wild approach with your creativity, there is no guarantee your creativity will impress a potential employer. Like art, your creativity can be interpreted differently by everyone. This is one of the risks you will need to factor in when developing your resume, delivering your elevator speech to an interviewer, or crafting your thank-you and follow-up letter.

An example of a wild and radical approach would be to include a graphic design and some artwork on your resume or going to a job interview with an outfit full of different colors. You may seem out of place if you are not going to an interview for a position in fashion or a position that relied heavily on your creativity and talent in art.

An example of a conservative approach would be to print your resume on plain white printer paper and going to the job interview in a traditional black-colored suit. This approach may seem boring, but it is the norm in American culture, so you should not worry about seeming out of place. However, this approach may not necessarily make you stand out from the crowd, either.

Your research prior to the interview plays a big role in your approach, from how you design your resume to answering interview questions. Find more about researching, storytelling, and adding value in Chapter 4.

Here are some questions you may be asked in a job interview to assess your creative attributes:
- Tell me about a time when you had to overcome a difficult problem.
- Tell me about a time when you went above and beyond what was expected of you.

- Give an example of a time when you dealt with a customer complaint.
- How did you handle your most challenging experience in your previous job?
- Tell me about how you worked effectively under pressure.
- Have you ever made a mistake? How did you handle it?
- Give an example of a goal you reached and tell me how you achieved it.
- Give an example of how you worked in a team.
- What do you do if you disagree with someone at work?
- Share an example of how you were able to motivate employees or coworkers.
- What are the steps you take for a project that requires the collection of systematic data- and risk-management in order to conduct a performance analysis?
- What are the steps you take to anticipate risks and resolve issues?

Improving your Thinking and Creativity

Although this book covers some of the many interview questions you may be asked, it is nearly impossible for you to memorize answers to all of them. A better approach is to tap into your creative side to come up with your own unique answers. This doesn't mean that there is no need to prepare for the interview. One of the biggest mistakes is going into a job interview unprepared.

Here are some other exercises you can do to improve and stimulate your thinking and creative skills.

- Read trade journals, reports, articles, nonfiction and fiction books. Read to stir your imagination and to spark the analytical side of your brain. Reading science-fiction and fantasy genres can also help stir your imagination. Some movies were based on these books, such as <u>Jurassic Park</u> by Michael Crichton. If you read the book and then watch the movie, compare how the author explains a scene or emotion in the book to how it's portrayed in the movie. Some movies based on books are filmed from the perspective and interpretation of the screenplay writer, costume designer, or even the producer.
- Analyze your professional strengths and weaknesses and think about what opportunities and threats exist because of those strengths and weaknesses. This exercise is similar to conducting a SWOT Analysis. You may be familiar with the SWOT analysis in marketing. Businesses use SWOT Analysis when developing their marketing strategies. You can use SWOT Analysis, as well, since you are marketing yourself to employers. Refer to "SWOT Analysis" in Chapter 6.
- Study problems a company dealt with through their case studies.
- Evaluate and learn from your experiences and the experiences of others.
- Learn from your past. Check on your progress. Review your calendar or journal.
- Put ideas and experiences into context.

- Ask questions about a problem; offer your ideas, and possible solutions.
- Surround yourself with others who challenge your thinking.
- Play board games that challenge the mind, such as chess.
- Play trivia games and pop-quiz games.

Make these exercises a consistent part of your life to continually improve. The more you practice, the more you will become
- Resourceful,
- Witty (thinking quickly on your feet), and
- Inventive.

Here are some suggested books to learn more about thinking quickly on your feet:

Are You Smart Enough to Work at Google? Trick Questions, Zen-like Riddles, Insanely Difficult Puzzles, and Other Devious Interviewing Techniques You Need to Know to Get a Job Anywhere in the New Economy by William Poundstone

Critical Thinking Skills Success in 20 Minutes a Day, 3rd Edition, by Learning Express

Thinking for a Change by John Maxwell

CHAPTER 11.

EMOTIONAL INTELLIGENCE

"Take control of your consistent emotions and begin to consciously and deliberately reshape your daily experience of life." -Tony Robbins

"Emotional intelligence (EI), is the capability of individuals to recognize their own emotions and those of others, discern between different feelings and label them appropriately, use emotional information to guide thinking and behavior, and manage and/or adjust emotions to adapt to environments or achieve one's goals."(1)

EI is a skill that requires being aware of and managing your emotions and your ability to recognize, cope with, and capitalize on the emotions of others. Managing your emotions and your mindset plays an important role. To improve your EI, you may consider taking anger- and stress-management courses. Self-awareness in this area is key to identifying and managing your emotions. Learn to improve on how you manage your emotions in certain situations. People respond and react with different levels of emotions to certain situations.

- Rejections
- Uninterested interviewers
- An irate customer
- An upset supervisor
- An uncooperative coworker
- Stress in the workplace or some type of unexpected event

In a job interview, you may be asked several behavioral types of questions to see how you react and respond to certain situations on the job.

- How would you deal with an irate customer?
- Tell me a time when you had a disagreement with your supervisor?
- How do you prioritize?
- If you were instructed by a supervisor to do something and then another told you to do something else, which supervisor you would you listen to first?

In some job interviews, you may be asked to perform simulations or role play with the interviewer so they can better assess how you handle certain situations.

The key to your ability to recognize, assess, and manage what you are feeling at that moment is your EI. It can take a thousandth of a second or it may take longer, depending on the individual and the situation involved. Some people say they can make decisions without involving their emotions, but every decision is made with emotions. You may stay calm in emergency situations and make rational decisions, but staying calm is an emotional response. It is an emotion that you can control with a certain level of intensity.

Handling Pressure & Criticism

I worked under great pressure a lot when I was in the Navy. One of those memorable moments was on 9/11/2001. I was assigned to Patrol Squadron Nine, based out of Hawaii but on deployment on Diego Garcia, an island somewhere in the middle of the Indian Ocean.

After working a twelve-hour shift, my buddy and I were at a nightclub, playing pool and relaxing. As we were playing, at about 7:00 pm local time, we watched the tragedy of a plane crashing into one of the twin towers in New York City on TV. Minutes later, we watched another plane crash into the other tower. Then the two towers collapsed. At that instant, we were all called to the hangar to be briefed by our Commanding Officer. At around 10:00 pm local time, he announced that we obtained intelligence that Osama Bin Laden and the terrorist group Al Qaeda were responsible for the attack. Our squadron was one of the first responders that people never knew about, working on the other side of the globe. Our mission was to fly over to Afghanistan on the hunt for Al Qaeda. However, some of our planes were not ready to fly due to multiple scheduled and unscheduled maintenance requirements. It was mission critical to get all our planes operational. A select of group of people from the day shift worked with the night shift to get our planes operational. There was a lot of pressure and adversity endured along the way. We were multi-tasking between several projects, handling problems as they arose, redoing tasks when things weren't done correctly the first time, jerry-rigging or improvising, and sometimes doing things manually when equipment did not function properly. Through all of that, we were also dealing with other people's frustrations and stress levels. We worked tirelessly and expeditiously to get our planes safe to fly.

Employers are looking for those employees who thrive under pressure and stay levelheaded in stressful situations. To see how you handle stressful and other situations, you may be asked several behavioral or scenario types of questions like:

- Give an example of a time you went above and beyond.
- Describe a time you helped solve a difficult problem.
- Describe a time you received constructive criticism.
- Describe a time you dealt with a customer complaint.
- Tell me about a time you had a disagreement with a coworker or supervisor.

At the interview, be levelheaded, have a positive attitude, display enthusiasm for the job and eagerness for challenges, demonstrate your ability to learn from mistakes and criticism, and demonstrate your commitment to overcome challenges.

Enthusiasm

Your enthusiasm affects your performance at work. Employers expect you to know what you are getting yourself into prior to even applying for the position. Employers get frustrated when they have to repost an open position because an employee quit after only working for a few weeks because of the stress and the difficulties that came with the job. To avoid this, employers want to know your level of enthusiasm for and commitment to the job and the company. You must do your research on what the job entails by thoroughly reading the job posting and the job description. Research more about the job and the company and reach out to any internal contacts you have for inside information.

At the interview, demonstrate your enthusiasm for the job, your eagerness for challenges, and your commitment to work through difficult times.

Here are some suggested books to learn more about emotional intelligence:

Emotional Intelligence: Practical Guide to Master Your Emotions, Improve Your Social Skills and Boost Your EQ for Business and Relationships | Overcome Anxiety and Unleash the Empath in You by Dr. Paul Sharp

Emotional Intelligence 2.0 by Travis Bradberry and Jean Greaves

Self-Scoring Emotional Intelligence Tests by Mark Daniel

CHAPTER 12.

ETHICAL VALUES & WORK ETHICS

"I follow three rules: Do the right thing, do the best you can, and always show people you care." -Lou Holtz

What are Ethics?

"Ethics or moral philosophy is a branch of philosophy that involves systematizing, defending, and recommending concepts of right and wrong conduct. Ethics seek to resolve questions of human morality by defining concepts such as good and evil, right and wrong, virtue and vice, justice and crime." (1)

What is right? What is wrong?

There are laws and company policies set in place to help determine which actions are right or wrong, legal or illegal. However, people have different belief systems and values, which guide them in deciding what to say or do in circumstances that lack such rules.

Ethical intelligence involves the value and belief systems that help you handle and solve problems. The decision to take an unethical action can not only lead to a possibly illegal action, but it can also create tension and uncomfortableness in the workplace. It can affect your reputation and even the company's.

Even though they are so important, it is not unusual to see companies shy away from discussing ethics.

Speaking about ethics can be a sensitive subject. Some people, and even some companies, have profited from unethical behavior, such as insider trading or sharing confidential information or trade secrets. You have heard of sexual harassment in the workplace environment: inappropriate relationships between a manager and his subordinates or abuse of professional authority, such as the Harvey Weinstein sexual abuse allegations. In government, you see news of a politician having been involved in a bribe. In education, you see news of cheating scandals. In fact, as of this writing, you are likely hearing about wealthy parents, some of whom are famous celebrities, who paid large sums of money as bribes to get their children into prestigious colleges.

When researching a company, look to see if they have their code of ethics and/or code of conduct posted publicly. Sometimes it is discussed within the company's values. Then research news articles and trade journals, preferably articles written by a third party not associated with the company, to see if the company had problems that involved ethics or if it is currently involved in ethics litigation.

Are your belief systems and values, including your ethical values, in alignment with the company's values and code of ethics?

Ethical Values

I spoke to a recruiter for the Transportation Security Administration (TSA) and questioned him about conducting credit checks on potential candidates. I was told that when they do so, they don't just look at credit scores. They look at a candidate's overall credit, work, and criminal history, among other things. It's like putting a jigsaw puzzle together. The report reveals a candidate's financial situation, as well as their motives and behaviors. It is understandable when a potential employee's credit score decreases when they have lost their job or had to foreclose on a house. But a candidate's level of responsibility can be determined by looking at whether the potential employee stopped making payments on his or her debt while employed, made late payments, or had accounts go into collections. Like an insurance company measures the risk of insuring you, companies measure your level of credit to determine the risk factor of hiring you. It helps determine whether you will act unethically during the performance of your job duties. For example, if someone applied to be a TSA agent at the airport while in dire financial distress, i.e. about to lose their house to foreclosure and become homeless, that person may be prone to accepting a bribe to allow contraband, illegal citizens or even a terrorist through airport security.

Thus, if you are a potential job candidate, a company may require you to take an ethics test. They may also require a drug test, credit check, and/or a criminal background check.

In the book, The Power of Ethical Management by Kenneth Blanchard and Norman Vincent Peale, it identifies the Ethics Check Questions we ask ourselves whenever we come across an ethical dilemma:
  1. "Is it legal? Will I be violating the company policies, code of ethics, standards of operating

procedures, etc.? Will I be violating any civil or criminal law?
2. Is it balanced? Is it fair to everyone in the short term and in the long term? Does it promote a win-win relationship?
3. How will it make me feel about myself? Will it make me feel proud? Will it allow me to have a clear conscience and not bother me? Will I feel good if my decision was publicly announced? Would I feel good if my family knew about it?" (2)

When our decisions bother us to the core, we feel guilty that we have compromised our own belief systems and values. It bothers us to the core that we may have a hard time sleeping, lose our appetite, and may be even embarrassed to share that experience with anyone. When we feel proud of our decisions that we made, we feel proud that we upheld to our belief systems and values. We may feel so proud that we may share our experience with others.

To learn more about The Five Principles of Ethical Power for Individuals and The Five Principles of Ethical Power for Organizations, refer to the book, <u>The Power of Ethical Management</u>.

Integrity & Honesty

"Integrity is the practice of being honest and showing a consistent and uncompromising adherence to strong moral and ethical principles and values." (3)

You may have read or heard about scandals in the news that involve compromising ethical values, integrity, and honesty. One such case was Enron. Now defunct, it was once a publicly traded energy company. It went bankrupt because the top executives of the company conducted unethical practices, among other things. They told the public to invest in the company while they were selling their own shares of stock, knowing that the company was not actually making a profit. To hide the losses, they had doctored their accounting and financial reports. A lot of people were hurt by these unethical practices.

To help avoid similar situations, companies may require a potential job candidate to undergo an ethics test along with a criminal background check. Here are some questions you may be asked in a job interview to assess your ethical values as well as your integrity, morals, and character traits.

- Describe three ethical values that you have.
- Have you ever stolen a pen at work?
- Give an example of a time you handled an issue of ethics or misconduct?
- Have you ever suffered in your career for doing what was right? Do you have any regrets?
- If your boss asked you to lie for him, what would you do?
- If you were in a situation where a coworker was doing something illegal or against company policy, what would you do?
- Tell me about a time you had a disagreement with a coworker or supervisor.
- Describe a time when you dealt with confidential information.

We talked about integrity and honesty in sales in Chapter 4. Remember that there are some preferred words you can use from the sales business to sell yourself in a positive way while still telling the truth. You can prove your honesty and integrity to someone you have just met by:

- Delivering on your first promise by showing up to the interview on time.
- Giving examples of your past work experiences and achievements where you demonstrated honesty, integrity, and delivered on your promises.
- Providing testimonials and Letters of Recommendation from references: those people you worked with and for, such as coworkers, managers, supervisors, and clients, who can vouch for your character.

Also, remember to be careful how much information you divulge. Providing too much information was covered in Chapter 1.

Work Ethics

"Working hard becomes a habit, a serious kind of fun. You get self-satisfaction from pushing yourself to the limit, knowing that all the effort is going to pay off." -Mary Lou Retton

What are Work Ethics?

"Work ethics are a set of values centered on importance of work and manifested by determination or desire to work hard. This value is considered to enhance character through hard work that is respective to an individual's field of work." (4)

It is important to point out that when you are describing your work ethics to employers, you will most likely describe some of your professional values and soft skills. Examples of such skills include being:

- Honest and Trustworthy
- Results Driven
- Goal Oriented
- A Perfectionist
- Customer-Focused
- A Professional

Exceeding Expectations

How do you exceed expectations when you haven't even started working yet? At the job interview, give examples and stories of your previous achievements to demonstrate what you can do for the new company. Note: such examples must be for the betterment of the company. Share results as proof of your performance. Examples:

- Recognized for increasing sales by 25%
- Rewarded for finding ways to cut costs or improve efficiencies
- Awarded for providing excellent customer service

You want to communicate to a potential employer how you are going to:

- Help solve problems,
- Meet their needs, and/or
- Help them make a decision.

Like getting your money's worth in making a big purchase, employers want to get their "bang for their buck" when they are looking for someone to join the company.

Here are some questions you may be asked in a job interview about your work ethics:
- Describe three ethical values that you have.
- What do you consider to be your most important work ethic?
- How would you describe your work ethic?

Here are some suggested books to learn more about ethical values and work ethics:

Business Ethics, 12th Edition, by O. C. Ferrell, John Fraedrich, and Linda Ferrell

The Ethical Warrior: Values, Morals and Ethics - For Life, Work and Service by Jack E. Hoban

The Power of Ethical Management by Kenneth Blanchard and Norman Vincent Peale

CHAPTER 13.

CUSTOMER SERVICE

"Customers are good for business." -Bill Walsh,
Business Coach

Your customer-service skills are important even if you are not applying for a customer-service position, per se. Every job candidate must have the traits to help and serve others. If you are providing a product or service, customers are involved, so serving customers is a requirement. In most professions, if not all, there are customers involved somewhere in the process. Without customers, a business could not survive. You may not think your job entails customer service, but you'd be surprised. If you work in HR, the employees of the company are your customers. If you are an Academic Instructor, your students are your customers. If you are hired to do market research for a company, that company is your customer. Whenever a profession deals with people, whether it's dealing with people in the organization or people outside of the organization, there are always customers.

Here are some questions an employer may ask you in a job interview to measure the level of your customer-service skills and experience:
- How do you handle a customer complaint?
- Explain a time when you dealt with a difficult customer.
- Tell me about a time when you delivered great customer service.

- Give an example of a time you went above and beyond for a customer.

Companies may provide training, as far as following certain protocols when dealing with customers and their complaints, but even without formal training you may already know some of the fundamentals of customer service. Customer service is no more than helping people, and you have been helping people for most of your life.

You offer help to a family member or a friend who has a problem. Similarly, at work, you offer help to customers or to the company that has a problem. One caveat: offer help with solutions that are actually within your capacity and within company policy. You may want to help a customer load their heavy furniture onto their truck, but you may not be able to do it yourself. You may find out that the company's liability coverage does not permit you to. Or you may not be able to offer a customer a complimentary item without a supervisor's approval. If you know you cannot help the customer, you should immediately refer them to an associate or someone else in the company who can. Do not string a customer along. This frustrates the customer more than had you not offered to help at all.

Even though a business may have company-specific policies, some procedures that are implemented when dealing with an irate customer are the fundamentals in customer service. In providing great customer service, applying your communication skills, especially in the areas of listening and building rapport, is critical. But you sometimes develop bad habits. Maybe you jump to conclusions and don't give the other person a chance to finish what they are saying or give them a chance to fully explain. Listening and staying calm in stressful situations are some of the most important traits to have when you are dealing with customers, especially irate customers. When a customer is irate, calm the person down so that you can have him or her explain the problem. They may be excessively frustrated or angry so they may just throw all kinds of complaints at you, instead of focusing on the issue at hand. Sometimes they just need a person to listen to them. If they feel they are being heard and know that you understand why they are frustrated or angry, it may alleviate some of their frustration even though, in the end, you may not be able to resolve the problem.

You should also ask customers for feedback. It is great to hear that a customer feels satisfied with the service that you provided. However, to learn and grow, you should also ask customers what else you or the company could have done better. Realize that you may not be able to please every customer but being open to new ideas and constructive criticism can help you and the company improve customer satisfaction and enhance customer service.

Here are some suggested books to learn more about customer service:

Be Our Guest: Perfecting the Art of Customer Service by the Disney Institute and Theodore Kinni

Customer Service for Dummies by Karen Leland and Keith Bailey

Raving Fans: A Revolutionary Approach to Customer Service by Ken Blanchard and Sheldon Bowles

CHAPTER 14.

MANAGEMENT & LEADERSHIP

"As a leader, the first person I need to lead is me. The first person that I should try to change is me." -John C. Maxwell

People often associate a job title that includes "management" with supervising and managing a staff. There are many different aspects of management, managing people is just one of them. Although you may not be applying for a supervisory role or management position, per se, employers do require you to have some management skills and leadership traits.

Taking the initiative by completing a task without being told and building rapport and motivating others on a team are some management and leadership traits you may possess and use on the job even without holding an official management title.

Here are some of the many different aspects of management:
- Personnel Management
- Human Resource Management
- Operations Management
- Project Management
- Program Management
- Time Management
- Anger Management
- Stress Management
- Change Management

- Risk Management
- Waste Management

In a job interview, to convince an employer you have what it takes to be a leader, give specific examples of how you applied your management and leadership skills in your prior position. Even though you may not be applying for a management or leadership position, showcase your leadership potential with the company. By the way, you do not have to be a manager to inspire and motivate others or to create a work environment that encourages teamwork and collaboration. If you are applying for a management position, expect to give examples of your leadership and management style.

Here are some questions an employer may ask to measure your management and leadership skills and experience:

- What do you expect from a manager?
- What do you find are the most difficult decisions to make?
- Tell me about a time when you were managing someone who had more experience in a specific area than you.
- Tell me about a time when you managed a problem employee.

Companies may provide training in management for those assuming a management or leadership role in the company, but even without formal training, you may already know some of the fundamentals of management. Management is no more than managing resources, which you have also done for most of your life. If you create a household budget, coordinate the family schedule, or hire babysitters for the kids, you have management skills. Managing time, people, and resources is a learned skill. Some people may look like a born leader but, more than likely, they built up that skill over time.

I applied many of the different aspects of management in my job when I started out as an Airman (Rank E-3) in the U.S. Navy. Eventually, I obtained a supervisory role as Petty Officer Second Class (E-5) and I learned to apply different management and leadership styles. I had to take a required leadership course when I took on the rank as an E-5 but learning to apply the things I learned from the course was a lot more difficult.

Look for ways to improve your management and leadership skills. If you are employed but are looking for other opportunities, ask your supervisor if it's possible to take on more responsibilities or a project. If you are in school, volunteer to be the leader for a team project or run for a leadership role in a club.

Volunteering or taking on a leadership role in a nonprofit organization or a professional association are also options. Joining a professional organization like Toastmasters can give you the opportunity to learn and gain leadership experience. Besides improving my speaking and communication skills, I joined Toastmasters to improve my leadership skills, as well. In Toastmasters, you gain leadership skills as Toastmaster of the Day, when you organize and lead a Toastmasters meeting. You can also assume a club officer role such as Vice President of Education or the President of the club.

Here are some suggested books to learn more about management and leadership:

Delivering Happiness: A Path to Profits, Passion, and Purpose by Tony Hsieh

Developing the Leader Within You by John C. Maxwell

Leaders Eat Last: Why Some Teams Pull Together and Other's Don't by Simon Sinek

Start with Why: How Great Leaders Inspire Everyone to Take Action by Simon Sinek

The Essential Workplace Conflict Handbook: A Quick and Handy Resource for Any Manager, Team Leader, HR Professional, or Anyone Who Wants to Resolve Disputes and Increase Productivity by Barbara Mitchell and Cornelia Gamlem

The One Minute Manager by Ken Blanchard and Spencer Johnson

CONCLUSION

"One of the exciting challenges in our lives is the challenge to better ourselves." -Robert Ritua

I hope this book has been helpful to you. I hope you have gained a better understanding of yourself and recognized your strengths, your positive qualities, and the areas you need to work on to improve your chances of acing your job interviews.

If you need further job coaching or even resume development, please contact me for a special price-discount offer for those of you who purchased this book.

I also would like to learn more about you. I welcome your feedback and would like to hear your experiences. I welcome you to visit my website and follow me in social media to share your experiences and to connect with and learn from other business professionals in the global community.

I wish you the best in your endeavors.

Sincerely,
Robert Ritua, MBA, Job Coach

NOTES

Introduction
1. Wikimedia Foundation, Inc. "Soft Skills." Wikipedia. Accessed October 27, 2019. https://en.wikipedia.org/wiki/Soft_skills

Part 1 Your Skills in Communication

Chapter 1. Attitude & Intrapersonal Communication Skills
1. Piper, Watty. The Little Engine That Could. New York, New York: Platt & Munk, 1930.

2. Walgreens. "Pharmacy Education Assistance Programs." Accessed on November 17, 2019. https://jobs.walgreens.com/education-assistance

3. U.S. Department of Veterans Affairs. "Education and Training." Accessed on November 17, 2019. https://www.benefits.va.gov/gibill/

4. U.S. Department of Veterans Affairs. "Veterans' Diseases Associated with Agent Orange." Accessed on November 17, 2019. https://www.publichealth.va.gov/exposures/agentorange/conditions/index.asp

5. U.S. Department of Veterans Affairs. "Gulf War Veterans' Illnesses." Accessed on November 17, 2019.

https://www.publichealth.va.gov/exposures/gulfwar/index.asp

6. U.S. Department of Veterans Affairs. "Public Health." Accessed on November 17, 2019. https://www.publichealth.va.gov/

7. Meyers, Nancy. "The Intern." DVD. Directed by Nancy Meyers. Los Angeles: Warner Brothers, 2015.

8. Avery, Beth and the National Employment Law Project (NELP). "Ban the Box: U.S. Cities, Counties, and States Adopt Fair Hiring Policies." Published by NLP. Updated July 1, 2019. https://www.nelp.org/publication/ban-the-box-fair-chance-hiring-state-and-local-guide/

9. U.S. Equal Employment Opportunity Commission. "What Employers Need to Know."

10. U.S. Equal Employment Opportunity Commission. "Pre-Employment Inquiries and Arrest & Conviction." Accessed October 27, 2019. https://www.eeoc.gov/laws/practices/inquiries_arrest_conviction.cfm

Chapter 2. Communication Skills

1. Branson, Richard. "You Can't Train a Smile." Virgin Group. Accessed October 28, 2019. https://www.virgin.com/richard-branson/you-cant-train-smile

2. Levy, Shawn and Vaughn, Vince. "The Internship." DVD. Directed by Shawn Levy. Los Angeles: 20th Century Fox, 2013.

Chapter 3. Interpersonal Communication & People Skills
1. Branson, Richard. "How I Hire: Focus on Personality." Virgin Group. Published September 23, 2013. https://www.linkedin.com/pulse/2013092323000 7-204068115-how-i-hire-focus-on-personality

2. Wikimedia Foundation, Inc. "DISC Assessment." Wikipedia. Accessed October 30, 2019. https://en.wikipedia.org/wiki/DISC_assessment

3. Wikimedia Foundation, Inc. "Holland Codes." Wikipedia. Accessed October 30, 2019. https://en.wikipedia.org/wiki/Holland_Codes

4. National Center for O*NET Development. "O*NET Interest Profiler." U.S. Department of Labor, Employment & Training Administration. Accessed October 31, 2019. https://www.mynextmove.org/explore/ip

5. Wikimedia Foundation, Inc. "Myers–Briggs Type Indicator." Wikipedia. Accessed October 31, 2019.https://en.wikipedia.org/wiki/Myers– Briggs_Type_Indicator

Chapter 4. Selling Skills
1. U.S. Securities and Exchange Commission. "Edgar Company Filings." n.d.

https://www.sec.gov/edgar/searchedgar/compan
ysearch.html

2. Bellino, Ricardo. You Have 3 Minutes! Learn
   the Secret of the Pitch from Trump's Original
   Apprentice. New York, New York: McGraw-Hill,
   2006.

3. Trump, Donald. Think Like a Billionaire. New
   York, New York: Random-House, 2004.

Chapter 8. Business Etiquette
1. Chaney, Lillian and Martin, Jeanette S. The
   Essential Guide to Business Etiquette.
   Westport, Connecticut: Greenwood Publishing,
   2006.

**Part 2 Other Important Professional Values & Soft
Skills**

Chapter 11. Emotional Intelligence
1. Wikimedia Foundation, Inc. "Emotional
   Intelligence." Wikipedia. Accessed November
   03, 2019.
   https://en.wikipedia.org/wiki/Emotional_intelligen
   ce

Chapter 12. Ethical Values & Work Ethics
1. Wikimedia Foundation, Inc. "Ethics." Wikipedia.
   Accessed November 03, 2019.
   https://en.wikipedia.org/wiki/Ethics

2. Blanchard, Kenneth and Vincent Peale, Norman. The Power of Ethical Management. New York, New York: William Morrow & Company, 1988.

3. Wikimedia Foundation, Inc. "Integrity." Wikipedia. Accessed November 03, 2019. https://en.wikipedia.org/wiki/Integrity

4. Wikimedia Foundation, Inc. "Work Ethic." Wikipedia. Accessed November 03, 2019. https://en.wikipedia.org/wiki/Work_ethic

ABOUT THE AUTHOR

ROBERT RITUA

✓ Loves making an impact in helping people, our community, and businesses create even more success.

✓ Offers diverse experience and a unique insight in business, investing, and life.

✓ Coach, Consultant, Trainer, Speaker, Author, Business Owner, Investor.

✓ Over 8 years Workforce Recruiting.

✓ Over 5 years Employment and Training/Case Management in Social Services.

✓ Also worked in various disciplines such as customer service, education, market research, real estate sales, investing and finance, food service, retail, health and fitness, quality assurance, safety, and aviation just to name a few.

✓ U.S. Navy Veteran: Over 10 years of service.

✓ Member of numerous professional associations including: Society for Human Resource Management (SHRM), The National Society of Leadership and Success (NSLS), and Toastmasters International.

✓ Volunteers at numerous non-profit organizations.

✓ Master's Degree in Business Administration.

NEED JOB COACHING?

Visit AceTheJobInterview.Win

If you need further job coaching or even resume development, please contact Robert Ritua for a special price discount offer for those of you who purchased this book.

Follow Robert Ritua in social media to share your experiences as well as to connect with and learn from other business professionals in the global community.

https://acethejobinterview.win/